Alfred Edward Woodley Mason

The Watchers

A Novel

Alfred Edward Woodley Mason

The Watchers
A Novel

ISBN/EAN: 9783337039370

Printed in Europe, USA, Canada, Australia, Japan

Cover: Foto ©ninafisch / pixelio.de

More available books at **www.hansebooks.com**

THE WATCHERS

A Novel

BY

A. E. W. MASON

AUTHOR OF "THE COURTSHIP OF MORRICE BUCKLER," ETC.

NEW YORK
FREDERICK A. STOKES COMPANY
PUBLISHERS

CONTENTS

CHAP.		PAGE
I.	TELLS OF A DOOR AJAR AND OF A LAD WHO STOOD BEHIND IT...	1
II.	DICK PARMITER'S STORY	17
III.	OF THE MAGICAL INFLUENCE OF A MAP	37
IV.	DESCRIBES THE REMARKABLE MANNER IN WHICH CULLEN MAYLE LEFT TRESCO	49
V.	THE ADVENTURE IN THE WOOD	64
VI.	MY FIRST NIGHT UPON TRESCO	81
VII.	TELLS OF AN EXTRAORDINARY INCIDENT IN CULLEN MAYLE'S BEDROOM	101
VIII.	HELEN MAYLE	110
IX.	TELLS OF A STAIN UPON A WHITE FROCK AND A LOST KEY	125
X.	IN WHICH I LEARN SOMETHING FROM AN ILL-PAINTED PICTURE	139
XI.	OUR PLANS MISCARRY UPON CASTLE DOWN	154
XII.	I FIND AN UNEXPECTED FRIEND	173
XIII.	IN THE ABBEY GROUNDS	192
XIV.	IN WHICH PETER TORTUE EXPLAINS HIS INTERVENTION ON MY BEHALF	203
XV.	THE LOST KEY IS FOUND	226
XVI.	AN UNSATISFACTORY EXPLANATION	238
XVII.	CULLEN MAYLE COMES HOME	250
XVIII.	MY PERPLEXITIES ARE EXPLAINED	265
XIX.	THE LAST	278

THE WATCHERS

CHAPTER I

TELLS OF A DOOR AJAR AND OF A LAD WHO STOOD BEHIND IT

I HAD never need to keep any record either of the date or place. It was the fifteenth night of July, in the year 1758, and the place was Lieutenant Clutterbuck's lodging at the south corner of Burleigh Street, Strand. The night was tropical in its heat, and though every window stood open to the Thames, there was not a man, I think, who did not long for the cool relief of morning, or step out from time to time on to the balcony and search the dark profundity of sky for the first flecks of grey. I cannot be positive about the entire disposition of the room: but certainly Lieutenant Clutterbuck was playing at ninepins down the middle with half a dozen decanters and a couple of silver salvers; and Mr. Macfarlane, a young gentleman of a Scottish regiment, was practising a game of his own.

He carried the fire-irons and Lieutenant Clutterbuck's sword under his arm, and walked solidly about the floor after a little paper ball rolled up out of a news sheet, which he hit with one of these instruments, selecting now the poker, now the tongs or the sword with great deliberation, and explaining his selection with even greater earnestness; there was besides a great deal of noise, which seemed to be a quality of the room rather than the utterance of any particular person; and I have a clear recollection that everything, from the candles to the glasses on the tables and the broken tobacco pipes on the floor, was of a dazzling and intolerable brightness. This brightness distressed me particularly, because just opposite to where I sat a large mirror hung upon the wall between two windows. On each side was a velvet hollow of gloom, in the middle this glittering oval. Every ray of light within the room seemed to converge upon its surface. I could not but look at it—for it did not occur to me to move away to another chair—and it annoyed me exceedingly. Besides, the mirror was inclined forward from the wall, and so threw straight down at me a reflection of Lieutenant Clutterbuck's guests, as they flung about the room beneath it.

Thus I saw a throng of flushed young exuberant faces, and in the background, continually peeping between them, my own, very white and drawn and thin and a million years old. That, too, annoyed me very much, and then by a sheer miracle, as it seemed to me, the mirror splintered and cracked and dropped in fragments on to the floor, until there was only hanging on the wall the upper rim, a thin curve of glass like a bright sickle. I remember that the noise and hurley-burley suddenly ceased, as though morning had come unawares upon a witches' carnival and that all the men present stood like statues and appeared to stare at me. Lieutenant Clutterbuck broke the silence, or rather tore it, with a great loud laugh which crumpled up his face. He said something about "Old Steve Berkeley," and smacked his hand upon my shoulder, and shouted for another glass, which he filled and placed at my elbow, for my own had disappeared.

I had no time to drink from it, however, for just as I was raising it to my lips Mr. Macfarlane's paper ball dropped from the ceiling into the liquor.

"Bunkered, by God!" cried Mr. Macfarlane, amidst a shout of laughter.

I looked at Macfarlane wth some reserve.

"I don't understand," I began.

"Don't move, man!" cried he, as he forced me back into my chair, and dropping the fire-irons with a clatter on to the floor, he tried to scoop the ball out of the glass with the point of Clutterbuck's sword-sheath. He missed the glass; the sheath caught me full on the knuckles; I opened my hand and——

"Sir, you have ruined my game," said Mr. Macfarlane, with considerable heat.

"And a good thing too," said I, "for a sillier game I never saw in all my life."

"Gentlemen," cried Lieutenant Clutterbuck, though he did not articulate the word with his customary precision; but his intentions were undoubtedly pacific. He happened to be holding the last of his decanters in his hand, and he swung it to and fro. "Gentlemen," he repeated, and as if to keep me company, he let the decanter slip out of his hand. It fell on the floor and split with a loud noise. "Well," said he, solemnly,

"I have dropped a brooch," and he fumbled at his cravat.

Another peal of laughter went up; and while it was still ringing, a man—what his name was I cannot remember, even if I ever knew it; I saw him for the first time that evening, and I have only once seen him since, but he was certainly more sober than the rest—stooped over my chair and caught me by the arm.

"Steve," said he, with a chuckle,—and from this familiarity to a new acquaintance I judge he was not so sober after all,—" do you notice the door?"

The door was in the corner of the room to my right. I looked towards it: the brass handle shone like a gold ball in the sun. I looked back at my companion, and, shaking my arm free, I replied coldly:

"I see it. It is a door, a mere door. But I do not notice it. It is not indeed noteworthy."

"It is unlatched," said my acquaintance, with another chuckle.

"I suppose it is not the only door in the world in that predicament."

"But it was latched a moment ago," and with his forefinger he gently poked me in the ribs.

"Then someone has turned the handle," said I, drawing myself away.

"A most ingenious theory," said he, quite unabashed by my reserve, "and the truth. Someone *has* turned the handle. Now who?" He winked with an extreme significance. "My dear sir, who?"

I looked round the room. Mr. Macfarlane had resumed his game. Two gentlemen in a corner through all the din were earnestly playing putt with the cards. They had, however, removed their wigs, and their shaven heads gleamed unpleasantly. Others by the window were vociferating the chorus of a drinking song. Lieutenant Clutterbuck alone was near to the door. I was on the point of pronouncing his name when he lurched towards it, and instantly the door was closed.

"It was someone outside," said I.

"Precisely. Steve, you are not so devoid of sense as your friends would have me believe," continued my companion. "Now, who will be Lieutenant Clutterbuck's timorous visitor?" He drew his watch from his fob: "We may hazard a guess at the sex, I think, but for the rest—— Is it some fine lady from St. James's who has come in her chair at half-past one of the morning to keep an appointment which her careless courtier has forgotten?"

"Hardly," I returned. "For your fine lady would hurry back to her chair with all the speed her petticoats allowed. She would not stay behind the door, which, I see, has again been opened."

The familiar stranger laid his hand upon my shoulder and held me back in my chair at arm's length from him.

"They do you wrong, my dear Steve," said he, gravely, "who say your brains are addled with drink. Your"—his tongue stumbled over a long word which I judged to be "ratiocination"—"is admirable. Never was logician more precise. It is not a fine lady from St. James's. It will be a flower-girl from Drury Lane, and may I be eternally as drunk as I am to-night, if we do not have her into the room."

With that he crossed the room, and seizing the handle suddenly swung the door open. The next instant he stepped back. The door was in a line with the wall against which my chair was placed, and besides it opened towards me so that I could not see what it was that so amazed him.

"Here's the strangest flower-girl from Drury

Lane that ever I saw," said he, and Lieutenant Clutterbuck turning about cried:

"By all that's wonderful, it's Dick Parmiter," and a lad of fifteen years, with a red fisherman's bonnet upon his head and a blue jersey on his back, stepped hesitatingly into the room.

"Well, Dick, what's the news from Scilly?" continued Clutterbuck. "And what's brought you to London? Have you come to see the king in his golden crown? Has Captain Hathaway lost his *Diodorus Siculus* and sent you to town to buy him another? Come, out with it!"

Dick shifted from one foot to another; he took his cap from his head and twisted it in his hands; and he looked from one to another of Lieutenant Clutterbuck's guests who had now crowded about the lad and were plying him with questions. But he did not answer the questions. No doubt the noise and the lights, and the presence of these glittering gentlemen confused the lad, who was more used to the lonely beaches of the islands and the companionable murmurs of the sea. At last he plucked up the courage to say, with a glance of appeal to Lieutenant Clutterbuck:

"I have news to tell, but I would sooner tell it to you alone."

His appeal was received with a chorus of protestations, and "Where are your manners, Dick," cried Clutterbuck, "that you tell my friends flat to their faces they cannot keep a secret?"

"Are we women?" asked Mr. Macfarlane.

"Out with your story," cried another.

Dick Parmiter shrank back and turned his eyes towards the door, but one man shut it to and leaned his shoulders against the panels, while the others caught at the lad's hesitation as at a new game, and crowded about him as though he was some rare curiosity brought by a traveller from outlandish parts.

"He shall tell his story," cried Clutterbuck. "It is two years since I was stationed at the Scilly Islands, two years since I dined in the messroom of Star Castle with Captain Hathaway of his Majesty's Invalids, and was bored to death with his dissertations on *Diodorus Siculus*. Two years! The boy must have news of consequence. There is no doubt trouble with the cray fish, or Adam Mayle has broken the head of the collector of the Customs House——"

"Adam Mayle is dead. He was struck down by paralysis and never moved till he died," interrupted Dick Parmiter.

The news sobered Clutterbuck for an instant. "Dead!" said he, gaping at the boy. "Dead!" he repeated, and so flung back to his noise and laughter, though there was a ring of savagery in it very strange to his friends. "Well, more brandy will pay revenue, and fewer ships will come ashore, and very like there'll be quiet upon Tresco——"

"No," interrupted Parmiter again, and Clutterbuck turned upon him with a flush of rage.

"Well, tell your story and have done with it!"

"To you," said the boy, looking from one to other of the faces about him.

"No, to all," cried Clutterbuck. The drink, and a certain anger of which we did not know the source, made him obstinate. "You shall tell it to us all, or not at all. Bring that table, forward, Macfarlane! You shall stand on the table Dick, like a preacher in his pulpit," he sneered, "and put all the fine gentlemen to shame, with a story of the rustic virtues."

The table was dragged from the corner into the middle of the room. The boy protested, and made for the door. But he was thrust back, seized and lifted struggling on to the table, where he was set upon his feet.

"Harmony, gentlemen, harmony!" cried Clutterbuck, flapping his hand upon the mantelshelf. "Take your seats, and no whispering in the side boxes, if you please. For I can promise you a play which needs no prologue to excuse it."

It was a company in which a small jest passed easily for a high stroke of wit. They applauded Lieutenant Clutterbuck's sally, and drew up their chairs round the table and sat looking upwards towards the boy, with a great expectation of amusement, just as people watch a bear-baiting at a fair. For my part I had not moved, and it was no doubt for that reason that Parmiter looked for help towards me.

"When all's said, Clutterbuck," I began, "you and your friends are a pack of bullies. The boy's a good boy, devil take me if he isn't."

The boy upon the table looked his gratitude for the small mercy of my ineffectual plea, and I should have proceeded to enlarge upon it had I not noticed a very astonishing thing. For Parmiter lifted his arm high up above his head as thought to impress upon me his gratitude, and his arm lengthened out and grew until it touched the ceiling. Then it dwindled and shrank until again it was no more than a boy's arm on a boy's shoulder. I was so struck with this curious phenomenon that I broke off my protest on his behalf, and mentioned to those about me what I had seen, asking whether they had remarked it too, and inquiring to what cause, whither of health or malady, they were disposed to attribute so sudden a growth and contraction.

However, Lieutenant Clutterbuck's guests were only disposed that night to make light of any subject however important or scientific. For some laughed in my face, others more polite, shrugged their shoulders with a smile, and the stranger who had spoken to me before clapped his hand in the small of my back as I leaned forward, and shouted some ill-bred word that, though might he die of small-pox if he had ever met me before, he would have known me from a thousand by the tales he had heard. However, before I could answer him fitly, and indeed, while I was still pondering the meaning of his words, Lieutenant Clutterbuck clapped his hands for silence, and Dick Parmiter, seeing no longer any hope of succour, perforce began to tell his story.

It was a story of a youth that sat in the stocks of a Sunday morning and disappeared thereafter from the islands; of a girl named Helen; of a negro who slept and slept, and of men watching a house with a great tangled garden that stood at the edge of the sea. Cullen Mayle, Parmiter called the youth who had sat in the stocks, son to that Adam whose death had so taken Lieutenant Clutterbuck with surprise. But I could not make head or tail of the business. For one thing I have always been very fond of flowers, and quite unaccountably the polished floor of the room blossomed into a parterre of roses, so that my attention was distracted by this curious and pleasing event.

For another, Parmiter's story was continually interrupted by intricate questions intended to confuse him, his evident anxiety was made the occasion of much amusement by those seated about the table, and he was induced on one excuse and another to go back to the beginning again and again and relate once more what he had already told. But I remember that he spoke with a high intonation, and rather quickly and with a broad accent, and that even then I was extremely sensible of the unfamiliar parts from which he came. His words seemed to have preserved a smell of the sea, and through them I seemed to hear very clearly the sound of waves breaking upon a remote beach—near in a word to that granite house with the tangled garden where the men watched and watched.

Then the boy's story ceased, and the next thing I heard was a sound of sobbing. I looked up, and there was Dick Parmiter upon the table, crying like a child. Over against him sat Lieutenant Clutterbuck, with a face sour and dark.

"I'll not stir a foot or lift a finger," said he, swearing an oath, "no, not if God comes down and bids me."

And upon that the boy weakened of a sudden, swayed for an instant upon his feet, and dropped in a huddle upon the table. His swoon put every one to shame except Clutterbuck; everyone busied himself about the boy, dabbing his forehead with wet handkerchiefs, and spilling brandy over his face in attempts to pour it into his mouth—every one except Clutterbuck, who never moved nor changed in a single line of his face, from his fixed expression of anger. Dick Parmiter recovered from his swoon and sat up: and his first look was towards the lieutenant, whose face softened for an instant with I know not what memories of days under the sun in a fishing boat amongst the islands.

"Dick, you are over-tired. It's a long road

from the Scillies to London. Very like, too, you are hungry," and Dick nodded "yes" to each sentence. "Well, Dick, you shall eat here, if there's any food in my larder, and you shall sleep here when you have eaten."

"Is that all?" asked Parmiter, simply, and Clutterbuck's face turned hard again as a stone.

"Every word," said he.

The boy slipped off the table and began to search on the ground. His cap had fallen from his hand when he fell down in his swoon. He picked it up from beneath a chair. He did not look any more at Clutterbuck; he made no appeal to anyone in the room; but though his legs still faltered from weakness, he walked silently out of the door, and in a little we heard his footsteps upon the stone stairs and the banisters creaking, as though he clung to them, while he descended, for support.

"Good God, Clutterbuck!" cried Macfarlane " he's but a boy."

"With no roof to his head," said another.

"And fainting for lack of a meal," said a third.

"He shall have both," I cried, "if he will take them from me," and I ran out of the door.

"Dick," I cried down the hollow of the staircase,

"Dick Parmiter," but no answer was returned, save my own cry coming back to me up the well of the stairs. Clutterbuck's rooms were on the highest floor of the house; the stone stairs stretched downwards flight after flight beneath me. There was no sound anywhere upon them; the boy had gone. I came back to the room. Lieutenant Clutterbuck sat quite still in his chair. The morning was breaking; a cold livid light crept through the open windows, touched his hands, reached his face and turned it white.

"Good-night," he said, without so much as a look.

His eyes were bent upon memories to which we had no clue. We left him sitting thus and went down into the street, when we parted. I saw no roses blossoming in the streets as I walked home, but as I looked in my mirror at my lodging I noticed again that my face was drawn and haggard and a million years old.

CHAPTER II

DICK PARMITER'S STORY

I WOKE up at mid-day, and lay for awhile in my bed anticipating wearily the eight limping hours to come before the evening fell, and wondering how I might best escape them. From that debate my thoughts drifted to the events of the night before, and I recollected with a sudden thrill of interest, rare enough to surprise me, the coming of Dick Parmiter, and his treatment at Clutterbuck's hands and his departure. I thought of his long journey to London along strange roads. I could see him tramping the dusty miles, each step leading him farther from that small corner of the world with which alone he was familiar. I imagined him now sleeping beneath a hedge, now perhaps, by some rare fortune, in one of Russell's waggons with the Falmouth mails, which at nightfall he had overtaken, and from which at daybreak he would descend with a hurried word of thanks to get the quicker on his way; I pictured him pressing through the towns with a growing fear at his heart, because of their turmoil and their crowds; and I thought of him as hungering daily more and more for the sea which he had left behind, like a sheep-dog which one has taken from the sheep and shut up within the walls of a city. The boy's spirit appealed to me. It was new, it was admirable; and I dressed that day with an uncommon alertness and got me out to Clutterbuck's lodgings.

I found the lieutenant in bed with a tankard of small ale at his bedside. He looked me over with astonishment.

"I wish I could carry my liquor as well as you do," said he, taking a pull at the tankard.

"Has the boy come back?" I asked.

"What, Dick?" said he. "No, nor will not." And changing the subject, "If you will wait, Steve, I will make a shift to get up."

I went into his parlour. The room had been put into some sort of order; but the shattered remnant of the mirror still hung between the windows, and it too spoke to me of Dick's journey. I imagined him coming to the great city at the fall of night, and seeking out his way through its alleys and streets to Lieutenant Clutterbuck's lodgings. I could see him on the stairs pausing to listen to the confusion within the rooms, and in the passage opening and closing the door as he hesitated whether to go in or no. I became all at once very curious to know what the errand was which had pushed him so far from his home, and I cudgelled my brains to recollect his story. But I could remember only the youth Cullen Mayle, who had sat in the stocks on a Sunday morning, and the girl Helen, and a negro who slept and slept, and a house with a desolate tangled garden by the sea, and men watching the house. But what bound these people and the house in a common history, as to that I was entirely in the dark.

"Steve," said Clutterbuck—I had not remarked his entrance—"you look glum as a November morning. Is it a sore head? or is it the sight of your mischievous handiwork?" and he pointed to the mirror.

"It's neither one nor the other," said I. "It's just the recollection of that boy fumbling under the table for his cap, and dragging himself silently out of the room, with all England to tramp and despair to sustain him."

"That boy!" cried Clutterbuck, with great

exasperation. "Curse you, Berkeley. That boy's a maggot, and has crept into your brains. We'll talk no more of him, if you please." He took a pack of cards from a corner cupboard, and, tossing them on the table, "Here, choose your game I'll play what you will, and for what stakes you will, so long as you hold your tongue."

It was plain that I should learn nothing by pressing my curiosity upon him. I must go another way to work. But chance and Lieutenant Clutterbuck served my turn without any provocation from myself.

I chose the game of picquet, and Clutterbuck shuffled and cut the cards; whereupon I dealt them. Clutterbuck looked at his hand fretfully, and then cried out:

"I have no hand for picquet, but I have very good putt cards."

I glanced through the cards I held.

"Make it putt, then," said I. "I will wager what you will my hand is the better;" and Clutterbuck broke into a laugh and tossed his cards upon the table.

"You have two kings and an ace," said he, "I know very well; but I have two kings and a deuce, and mine are the better."

"It is a bite," said I.

"And an ingenious one," he returned. "It was Cullen Mayle who taught it to us in the mess at Star Castle. For packing the cards or knapping the dice I never came across his equal. Yet we could never detect him, and in the end not a soul in the garrison would play with him for crooked pins."

"Cullen Mayle," said I; "that was Adam's son."

Clutterbuck had sunk into something of a reverie, and spoke rather to himself than to me.

"They were the strangest pair," he continued; "you would never take them for father and son, and I myself was always amazed to think there was any relationship between them. I have seen them sitting side by side on the settle in the kitchen of the "Palace Inn" at Tresco. Adam, an old bulky fellow, with a mulberry face and yellow angry eyes, and his great hands and feet twisted out of all belief. His stories were all of wild doings on the Guinea coast. Cullen, on the other hand, was a stripling with a soft face like a girl's, exquisite in his dress, urbane in his manners. He had a gentle word and an attentive ear for each newcomer to the fire, and a white protesting hand for the oaths with which Adam salted his speech. Yet they were both of the same vindictive, turbulent spirit, only Cullen was the more dangerous.

"I have watched the gannets often through an afternoon in Hell Bay over at Brehar. They would circle high up in the air where no fish could see them, and then slant their wings and drop giddily with the splash of a stone upon their prey. They always put me in mind of Cullen Mayle. He struck mighty quick and out of the sky. I cannot remember, during all the ten years I lived at the Scillies, that any man crossed Cullen Mayle, though unwittingly, but some odd accident crippled him. He was the more dangerous of the pair. With Adam it was a word and a blow. With Cullen a word and another and another, and all of them soft, and the blow held over for a secret occasion. But it fell. If ever you come across Cullen Mayle, Berkeley, take care of your words and your deeds, for he strikes out of the sky and mighty quick."

This Clutterbuck said with an extreme earnestness, leaning forward to me as he spoke. And even now I can but put it down to his earnestness that a shiver took me at the words; for nothing was more unlikely than that I should ever come to grips with Cullen Mayle, and the next moment I answered Clutterbuck lightly.

"Yet he sat in the stocks in the end," said I, with as much indifference as I could counterfeit; for I was afraid lest any display of eagerness might close his lips. Lieutenant Clutterbuck, however, was hardly aware that he was being questioned. He laughed with a certain pleasure.

"Yes. A schooner, with a cargo of brandy, came ashore on Tresco. Cullen and the Tresco men saved the cargo and hid it away, and when the collector came over with his men from the Customs House upon St. Mary's, Cullen drove him back to his boats with a broken head. Cullen broke old Captain Hathaway's patience at the same time. Hathaway took off his silver spectacles at last and shut up his *Diodorus Siculus* with a bang; and so Cullen Mayle sat in the stocks before the Customs House on the Sunday morning. He left the islands that night. That was two years and a month ago."

"And what had Dick Parmiter to do with Cullen Mayle?" said I.

"Dick?" said he. "Oh, Dick was Cullen

Mayle's henchman. But it seems that Dick has transferred his allegiance to——" And he stopped abruptly. His face soured as he stopped.

"To the girl Helen?" said I, quite forgetting my indifference.

"Yes!" cried Clutterbuck, savagely, "to the girl Helen. He is fifteen years old is Dick. But at fifteen years a lad is ripe to be one of Cupid's April fools." And after that he would say no more.

His last words, however, and, more than his words, the tone in which he spoke, had given me the first definite clue of the many for which my curiosity searched. It was certainly on behalf of the girl, whom I only knew as Helen, that Dick had undertaken his arduous errand, and it was no less certain that just for that reason Lieutenant Clutterbuck had refused to meddle in the matter. I recognised that I should get no advantage from persisting, but I kept close to his side that day waiting upon opportunity.

We dined together at Locket's, by Charing Cross; we walked together to the "Cocoa Tree" in St. James's Street, and passed an hour or so with a dice-box. Clutterbuck was very silent for the most part. He handled the dice-box with indifference; and, since he was never the man to keep his thoughts for any long time to himself, I had no doubt that some time that day I should learn more. Indeed, very soon after we left the "Cocoa Tree" I thought the whole truth was coming out; for he stopped in St. James's Park, close to the Mall, which at that moment was quiet and deserted. We could hear a light wind rippling through the leaves of the poplars, and a faint rumble of carriages lurching over the stones of Pall Mall.

"It is very like the sound of the sea on a still morning of summer," said he, looking at me with a vacant eye, and I wondered whether he was thinking of a tangled garden raised above a beach of sand, wherein, maybe, he had walked, and not alone on some such day as this two years ago.

We crossed the water to the Spring Gardens at Vauxhall, where we supped. I was now fallen into as complete a silence and abstraction as Clutterbuck himself, for I was clean lost in conjectures. I knew something now of Adam Mayle and his son Cullen, but as to Helen I was in the dark. Was her name Mayle too? Was she wife to Cullen? The sight of Clutterbuck's ill-humour inclined me to that conjecture; but I was wrong, for as the attendants were putting out the lights in the garden I ventured upon the question. To my surprise, Clutterbuck answered me with a smile.

"Sure," said he, "you are the most pertinacious fellow. What's come to you, who were content to drink your liquor and sit on one side while the world went by? No, she was not wife to Cullen Mayle, nor sister. She was a waif of the sea. Adam Mayle picked her up from the rocks a long while since. It was the only action that could be counted to his credit since he came out of nowhere and leased the granite house of Tresco. A barque—a Venetian vessel, it was thought, from Marseilles, in France, for a great deal of Castile soap, and almonds and oil was washed ashore afterwards—drove in a northwesterly gale on to the Golden Bar reef. The reef runs out from St. Helen's Island, opposite Adam Mayle's window. Adam put out his lugger and crossed the sound, but before he could reach St. Helen's the ship went down into fourteen fathoms of water. He landed on St. Helen's, however, and amongst the rocks where the reef joins the land he came across a sailor, who lay in the posture of death, and yet wailed like a hungry child. The sailor was dead, but within his jacket, buttoned up on his breast, was a child of four years or so. Adam took her home. No one ever claimed her, so he kept her, and called her Helen from the island on which she was wrecked. That was a long time since, for the girl must be twenty."

"Is she French?" I asked.

"French, or Venetian, or Spanish, or what you will," he cried. "It matters very little what country a woman springs from. I have no doubt that a Hottentot squaw will play you the same tricks as a woman of fashion, and with as demure a countenance. Well, it seems we are to go to bed sober;" and we went each to his lodging.

For my part, I lay awake for a long time, seeking to weave into some sort of continuous story what I had heard that day from Lieutenant Clutterbuck and the scraps which I remembered of Parmiter's talk. But old Adam Mayle, who was dead; Cullen, the gannet who struck from the skies; and even Helen, the waif of the sea—these were at this time no more to me than a showman's puppets; marionettes of sawdust and wood, that faced this way and that way according as I pulled the strings. The one being who had life was the boy Parmiter, with his jersey and his red fisherman's bonnet; and I very soon turned to conjecturing how he fared upon his journey.

Had he money to help him forward? Had he fallen in with a kindly carrier? How far had he travelled? I had no doubt that, whether he had money or no, he would reach his journey's end. His spirit was evident in the resolve to travel to London, in his success, and in the concealment of any weakness until the favour he asked for had been refused.

I bought next morning one of the new maps of the Great West Road and began to pick off the stages of his journey. This was the second day since he had started. He would not travel very fast, having no good news to lighten his feet. I reckoned that he would have reached the "Golden Farmer," and I made a mark at that name on the map. Every day for a week I kept in this way an imagined tally of his progress, following him from county to county; and at the end of the week, coming out in the evening from my lodging at the corner of St. James's Street, I ran plump into the arms of the gentleman I had met at Clutterbuck's, and whose name I did not know. But his familiarity was all gone from him. He bowed to me stiffly, and would have passed on, but I caught him by the arm.

"Sir," said I, "you will remember a certain night when I had the honour of your acquaintance."

"Mr. Berkeley," he returned with a smile, "I remember very much better the dreadful morning which followed it."

"You will not, at all events, have forgotten the boy whom you discovered outside the door, and if you can repeat the story which he told, or some portion of it, I shall be obliged to you."

He looked at his watch.

"I have still half an hour to spare," said he; and he led the way to the "Groom Porters." The night was young, but not so young but what the Bassett-table was already full. We sat down together in a dark corner of the room, and my companion told me what he remembered of Parmiter's story.

It appeared that Cullen Mayle had quarrelled with his father on that Sunday night after he had sat in the stocks and had left the house. He had never returned. A year ago Adam Mayle had died, bequeathing his fortune, which was considerable, and most of it placed in the African Company, to his adopted daughter Helen. She, however, declared that she had no right to it, that it was not hers, and that she would hold it in trust until such time as Cullen should come back to claim it.

He did not come back, as has been said; but eight months later Dick Parmiter, on an occasion when he had crossed in his father's fishing boat to Cornwall, had discovered upon Penzance Quay a small crowd of loiterers, and on the ground amongst them, with his back propped against a wall, a negro asleep. A paper was being passed from hand to hand among the group, and in the end it came to Dick Parmiter. Upon the paper was written Adam Mayle's name and the place of his residence, Tresco, in the Scilly Islands; and Dick at once recognised that the writing was in Cullen Mayle's hand. He pushed to the front of the group, and stooping down, shook the negro by the shoulder. The negro drowsily opened his eyes.

"You come from Mr. Cullen Mayle?" said Dick.

"Yes," said the negro, speaking in English and quite clearly.

"You have a message from him?"

"Yes."

"What is it?" asked Dick; and he put a number of questions eagerly. But in the midst of them, and while still looking at Dick, the negro closed his eyes deliberately and fell asleep.

"See," cried a sailor, an oldish white-haired man, with a French accent; "that is the way with him. He came aboard with us at the port of London as wide awake as you or I. Bound for Penzance he was, and the drowsiness took him the second day out. At first he would talk a little; but each day he slept more and more, until now he will say no more than a 'Yes' or a 'No.' Why, he will fall asleep over his dinner."

Dick shook the negro again.

"Do you wish to cross to Tresco?"

"Yes," said the negro.

Dick carried him back to Scilly and brought him to the house on Tresco, where Helen Mayle now lived alone. But no news could be got from him. He would answer "Yes" or "No" and eat his meals; but when it came to a question of his message or Cullen Mayle's whereabouts he closed his eyes and fell asleep. Helen judged that somewhere Cullen was in great need and distress, and because she held his money, and could do nothing to succour him, she was thrown into an extreme trouble. There was some reason why he could not come to Scilly in person, and here at her hand was the man sent to tell the reason; but he could not because of his mysterious malady. More than once he tried with a look of deep sadness in his eyes, as though he was conscious of his helplessness, but he never got beyond the first word. His eyelids closed while his mouth was still open to speak, and at once he was asleep. His presence made a great noise amongst the islands; from Brehar, from St. Mary's, and from St. Martin's the people sailed over to look at him. But Helen, knowing Cullen Mayle and fearing the nature of his misadventure, had bidden Parmiter to let slip no hint that he had come on Cullen's account.

So the negro stayed at Tresco and spread a great gloom throughout the house. They watched him day by day as he slept. Cullen's need might be immediate; it might be a matter of crime; it might be a matter of life and death. The gloom deepened into horror, and Helen and her few servants, and Dick, who was much in the house, fell into so lively an apprehension that the mere creaking of a door would make them start, a foot crunching on the sand outside sent them flying to the window. So for a month, until Dick Parmiter, coming over the hill from New Grimsby harbour at night, had a lantern flashed in his face, and when close to the house saw a man spring up from the gorse and watch him as he passed. From that night the house was continually spied upon, and Helen walked continually from room to room wringing her hands in sheer distraction at her helplessness. She feared that they were watching for Cullen; she feared, too, that Cullen, receiving no answer to his message, would come himself and fall into their hands. She dared hardly conjecture for what reason they were watching, since she knew Cullen. For a week these men watched, five of them, who kept their watches as at sea; and then Dick, taking his courage in his hands, and bethinking him of Lieutenant Clutterbuck, who had been an assiduous visitor at the house on Tresco, had crossed over to St. Mary's and learned from old Captain Hathaway where he now lived. He had said nothing of his purpose to Helen, partly from a certain shyness at speaking to her upon a topic of some delicacy, and partly lest he should awaken her hopes and perhaps only disappoint them. But he had begged a passage in a ship that was sailing to Cornwall, and, crossing thither secretly, had made his way in six weeks to London.

This is the story which my acquaintance repeated to me as we sat in the "Groom Porters."

"And Clutterbuck refused to meddle in the matter," said I. "Poor lad!"

I was thinking of Dick, but my companion mistook my meaning, for he glanced thoughtfully at me for a second.

"I think you are very right to pity him," he said; "although, Mr. Berkeley, if you will pardon me, I am a trifle surprised to hear that sentiment from you. It is indeed a sodden, pitiful, miserable dog's life that Clutterbuck leads. To pass the morning over his toilette, to loiter through the afternoon in a boudoir, and to dispose of the evening so that he may be drunk before midnight! He would be much better taking the good air into his lungs and setting his wits to unknot that tangle amongst those islands in the sea. But I have overstayed my time. If you can persuade him to that, you will be doing him no small service;" and politely taking his leave, he went out of the room.

I sat for some while longer in the corner. I

could not pretend that he had spoken anything but truth, but I found his words none the less bitter on that account. A pitiful dog's life for Lieutenant Clutterbuck, who was at the most twenty-four years of age! What, then, was it for me, who had seven years the better of Lieutenant Clutterbuck, or rather, I should say, seven years the worse? I was thirty-one that very month, and Clutterbuck's sodden, pitiful life had been mine for the last seven years. An utter disgust took hold of me as I repeated over and over to myself my strange friend's words. I looked at the green cloth and the yellow candles, and the wolfish faces about the cloth. The candles had grown soft with the heat of the night, and were bent out of their shape, so that the grease dropped in great blots upon the cloth, and the air was close with an odour of stale punch. I got up from my corner and went out into the street, and stood by the water in St. James's Park. If only some such summons had come to me when I was twenty-four as had now come to Clutterbuck!—well, very likely I should have turned a deaf ear to it, even as he had done! And—and, at all events, I was thirty-one and the summons had not come to me, and there was an end of the matter. To-morrow I should go back to the green cloth and not trouble my head about the grease blots; but to-night, since Clutterbuck was twenty-four, I would try to do him that small service of which the stranger spoke, and so setting out at a round pace I made my way to Clutterbuck's lodging.

CHAPTER III

OF THE MAGICAL INFLUENCE OF A MAP

I DID not, however, find Lieutenant Clutterbuck that night. He was out of reach, and likely to remain so for some while to come. He had left his lodgings at mid day and taken his body-servant with him, and his landlady had no knowledge of his whereabouts. I thought it probable, however, that some of his friends might have that knowledge, and I thereupon hurried to those haunts where of an evening he was an habitual visitor. The "Hercules Pillars" in Piccadilly, the "Cocoa Tree" in St. James's Street, the "Spring Gardens" at Vauxhall, "Barton's" in King Street, the "Spread Eagle" in Covent Garden,—I hurried from one to the other of these places, and though I came upon many of Clutterbuck's intimates, not one of them was a whit better informed than myself. I returned to my lodging late and more disheartened than I could have believed possible in a matter wherein I had no particular concern. And, indeed, it was not so much any conjecture as to what strange tragical events might be happening about that watched and solitary house in Tresco which troubled me, or even pity for the girl maddened by her fears, or regret that I had not been able to do Clutterbuck that slight service which I purposed. But I took out the map of the Great West Road, and thought of the lad Parmiter trudging along it, doing a day's work here among the fields, begging a lift there upon a waggon and slowly working his way down into the West. I had a very clear picture of him before my eyes. The day was breaking, I remember, and I blew out the candles and looked out of the window down the street. The pavement was more silent at that hour than those country roads on which he might now be walking, or that hedge under which he might be shaking the dew from off his clothes. For there the thrush would be calling to the blackbird with an infinite bustle and noise, and the fields of corn would be whispering to the fields of wheat.

I came back again to my map, and while the light broadened, followed Parmiter from the outset of his journey, through Knightsbridge, along the Thames, between the pine-trees of Hampshire, past Whitchurch, and into the county of Devon. The road was unwound before my eyes like a tape. I saw it slant upwards to the brow of a hill, and dip into the cup of a valley; here through a boskage of green I saw a flash of silver where the river ran; there between flat green fields it lay, a broad white line geometrically straight to the gate of a city; it curved amongst the churches and houses, but never lost itself in that labyrinth, aiming with every wind and turn at that other gate, from which it leaped free at last to the hills. And always on the road I saw Dick Parmiter, drunk with fatigue, tottering and stumbling down to the West.

For awhile he occupied that road alone; but in the end I saw another traveller a long way behind —a man on horseback, who spurred out from London and rode with the speed of the wind. For a little I watched that rider, curious only to discern how far he travelled, and whether he would pass Dick Parmiter; then, as I saw him drawing nearer and nearer, devouring the miles which lay between, it came upon me slowly that he was riding not to pass but to overtake; and at once the fancy flashed across me that this was

Clutterbuck. I gazed at my map upon the table as one might gaze into a magician's globe. It was no longer a map; it was the road itself imprisoned in hedges, sunlit, and chequered with the shadows of trees. I could see the horseman, I could see the dust spirting up from beneath his horse's hoofs like smoke from a gun-barrel. Only his hat was pushed down upon his brows because of the wind made by the speed of his galloping, so that I could not see his face. But it was Clutterbuck I had no doubt. Whither had he gone from his lodging? Now I was convinced that I knew. There had been no need of my night's wanderings from tavern to tavern, had I but looked at my map before. It was Clutterbuck without a doubt. At some bend of the road he would turn in his saddle to look backwards, and I should recognise his face. It was Lieutenant Clutterbuck, taking the good air into his lungs with a vengeance. He vanished into a forest, but beyond the forest the road dipped down a bank of grass and lay open to the eye. I should see him in a second race out, his body bent over his horse's neck to save him from the swinging boughs. I could have clapped my hands with sheer pleasure. I wished that my voice could have reached out to Parmiter, tramping wearily so far beyond; in my excitement, I believed that it would, and before I knew what I did, I cried out aloud :

"Parmiter! Parmiter!" and a voice behind me answered :

"You must be mad, Berkeley! What in the world has come to you?"

I sat upright in my chair. The excitement died out of me and left me chilly. I looked about me; I was in my own lodging at the corner of St James's Street, outside in the streets the world was beginning to wake, and the voice which had spoken to me and the hand which was now laid upon my shoulder were the voice and the hand of Lieutenant Clutterbuck.

"What's this?" said he, leaning over my shoulder. "It is a map."

"Yes," I answered, "it is a mere map, the map of the Great West Road;" and in my eyes it was no longer any more than a map.

Clutterbuck, who was holding it in his hand, dropped it with a movement and an exclamation of anger. Then he looked curiously at me, stepped over to the sideboard and took up a glass or two which stood there. The glasses were clean and dry. He looked at me again, his curiosity had grown into uneasiness; he walked to the opposite side of the table, and drawing up a chair seated himself face to face with me.

"I hoped you were drunk," said he. "But it seems you are as sober as a bishop. Are you daft, then? Has it come to a strait-waistcoat? I come back late from Twickenham. I stopped at the Hercules Pillars." There I heard that you had rushed in two hours before in a great flurry and disorder, crying out that you must speak to me on the instant. The same story was told to me at the 'Cocoa Trees.' My landlady repeated it. I conjectured that it must needs be some little affair to be settled with sharps at six in the morning; and so that you might not say your friends neglect you, I turn from my bed, and hurry to you at three o'clock of the morning. I find that you have left your front-door unlatched for any thief that wills to make his profit of the house. I come into your room and find you bending over a map in a great excitement and crying out aloud that damned boy's name. Is he to trouble my peace until the Judgment Day? Are you daft, eh, Steve?" and he reached his hand across the table not unkindly, and laid it on my sleeve. Are you daft?"

I was staring again at the map, and did not answer him. He shifted his hand from my sleeve and took it up and away from my eyes. He looked at it himself, and then spoke slowly, and in quite a different voice:

"It is a curious, suggestive thing, the map of a road, when all's said," he observed slowly. "I'll not deny but what it seizes one's fancies. Its simple lines and curves call up I know not what pictures of flowering hedgerows; a little black blot means a village of stone cottages, very likely overhung with ivy and climbed upon with roses." He suddenly thrust the map again under my nose, "What do you see upon the road?" said he.

"Parmiter," I answered.

"Of course," he interrupted sharply. "Well, where is Parmiter?" and I laid a finger on the map.

"Between Fenny Bridges and Exeter," said he, leaning forward. "He has made great haste."

He spoke quite seriously, not questioning my conjecture, but accepting it as a mere statement of fact.

"That is a heath?" he asked, pointing to an inch or so where the map was shaded on each side of the high-road. "Yes, a heath t'other side of

Hartley Row; I know it. There should be a mail-coach there, and the horses out of the shafts, and one or two men in crape masks and a lady in a swoon, and the driver stretched in the middle of the road with a bullet through his crop."

"I do not see that," I returned. "But here, beyond Axminster———"

"Well?"

He leaned yet further forward.

"There is a forest here."

"Yes."

"I saw a man on horseback ride into it between the trees. He has not as yet emerged from it."

"Who was he? Did you know him?"

"I thought I did. But I could not see his face."

Clutterbuck watched that forest eagerly, and with a queer suspense in his attitude and even in his breathing. Every now and then he raised his eyes to mine with a question in them. Each time I shook my head, and answered:

"Not yet," and we both again stared at the map.

Then Clutterbuck whispered quickly:

"What if his horse had stumbled? What if he is lying there at the roadside beneath the tree?"

MAGICAL INFLUENCE OF A MAP

He tore himself away from the contemplation of the map. "The thing's magical!" he cried. "It has bewitched you, Steve, and by the Lord it has come near to bewitching me!"

"I thought the horseman was yourself. Why don't you go?" said I, pointing to the map.

Lieutenant Clutterbuck rose impatiently from his chair.

"There must be an end of this. Once for all I will not go. There is no reason I should. There is reason why I should not. You do not know in what you are meddling. You are taken like a schoolboy by an old wife's tale of a lonely girl trapped in a net. You are too old for such follies."

"I was too old a fortnight ago," I returned, "but, by the Lord, these last days I have grown young again—so young that——"

I stopped suddenly. Not until this instant had the notion occurred to me, but it came now, it thrilled through me with a veritable shock. I leaned back in my chair and stared at Clutterbuck. He understood, for he in his turn stared at me.

"The rider!" said he breathlessly, tapping the map with his forefinger, "the man whose face you did not see!"

I nodded at him.

"What if the face were mine?" said I.

"You could never believe it."

"I believe that I have even enough youth for that," I cried, and I bent over the map, trying again to fashion from its plain black and white my picture of the great high-road, climbing and winding through a country-side rich with all the colours of the summer. But it was only a map of lines and curves, nor could I any longer discover the horseman who spurred along it—though I had now a particular reason to wish for a view of his face,—or the wood into which he disappeared.

"Well, has your cavalier galloped into the open yet?" asked Clutterbuck.

He spoke with sarcasm, but the sarcasm was forced. It was but a cloak to cover and excuse the question.

I shook my head.

"No, and he will not," said Clutterbuck.

"Is that so sure?" I asked. "What if the face were mine?"

"You are serious!" he cried. "You would go a stranger and offer your unsought aid? It would be an impertinence."

"Suppose life and death are in the balance, would they weigh impertinence?"

"It might be *your* life and *your* death!"

And as he spoke, it seemed to me that all my last seven years rose up in their shrouds and laughed at him.

"And what then?" I cried. "Would the world shiver if I died? Would even a tavern-keeper draw down his blinds? Perhaps some drunkard in his cups would wish I lived, that he might take my measure in a drinking-bout. There's my epitaph for you! Good Lord, Clutterbuck, but I would dearly love to die a clean death! There's that boy Parmiter tramping down his road. He does a far better thing than I have ever done. You know! Why talk of it? You know the life I have lived, and since that boy flung his example in my eyes, upon my word I sicken to think of it. Twelve years ago, Clutterbuck, I came to London, a cadet with a cadet's poor portion, but what a wealth of dreams! A fortune first, if I slaved till I was forty, and then I would set free my soul and live! The fortune came, and I slaved but six years for it. The treaty of Aix and a rise of stocks, and there was my fortune. You know how I have lived since."

Clutterbuck looked at me curiously. I had never said so much to him or to any man in this strain. Nor should I have said so much now, but I was fairly shaken out of my discretion. For a little Clutterbuck sat silent and motionless. Then he said gently:

"Shall I tell you why I will not go? Yes, I will tell you," and he told me the history of that Sunday, two years ago, when Cullen Mayle sat in the stocks, or at least as much of it as had come within his knowledge. The events of that day were the beginning of all the trouble, indeed, but Lieutenant Clutterbuck never knew more of it than what concerned himself, and as I sat over against him on that July morning and listened to his story while the world awoke, I had no suspicion of what the passage of that Sunday hid, or of the extraordinary consequences which it brought about.

CHAPTER IV

DESCRIBES THE REMARKABLE MANNER IN WHICH CULLEN MAYLE LEFT TRESCO

"It was my business," he began, "to fetch Cullen Mayle from Tresco over to St. Mary's where the stocks were set. It was an unpleasant business, and to me doubly and damnably unpleasant."

"I understand!" said I, thinking of how he had before spoken to me of Adam Mayle's adopted daughter.

"I took a file of Musquets, found the three of them at breakfast, and, with as much delicacy as I could, explained my errand. Helen alone showed any distress or consciousness of disgrace. Cullen strolled to the window, and seeing that I had placed my men securely about the house and that my boat was ready on the sand not a dozen yards away, professed himself, with an inimitable indifference, willing to gratify my wishes;

while Adam, so far from manifesting any anger, broke out into a great roar of laughter.

"'Cullen, my boy,' he shouted, like a man highly pleased, 'here's a nasty stumble for your pride. To sit in the stocks of a Sunday morning, when all the girls can see you as they come from church! To sit in the stocks like a common drunkard; and you that sets up for a gentleman! Oh, Cullen, Cullen!' He wagged his head from side to side, and so brought his fist upon the table with a bang which set all the plates dancing. 'Devil damn me,' said he, 'if I don't sail to church at St. Mary's myself and see how you look in your wooden garters.' Cullen glanced carelessly towards me. 'An unseemly old man,' said he; and we left Adam still shaking like a monstrous jelly-fish, and crossed back to St. Mary's from Tresco.

"Sure enough Adam kept his word. They were singing the *Nunc Dimittis* in the church when Adam stumped up the aisle. He had brought Helen with him, and she looked as though she wished the brick floor to open and let her out of sight. But Adam kept his head erect and showed a face of an extraordinary good humour. You may be certain that the parson got the scantiest attention imaginable to his discourse. For one thing,

Adam Mayle had never set foot in St. Mary's Church before, and for another, every one was agog to see how he would bear himself afterwards, when he passed on his way to the quay across the little space before the Customs House.

"There was a rush to the church door as soon as the benediction was pronounced, and it happened that I was one of the last to come out of the porch. The first thing that I saw was Adam walking a little way apart amongst the gravestones with a stranger, and the next thing, Helen talking to Dick Parmiter."

Here I interrupted Clutterbuck, for I was anxious to let no detail escape me.

"Had Dick crossed with Adam Mayle from Tresco?"

"I think not," returned Clutterbuck. "He was not in the church. I do not know, but I fancy he brought the stranger over to St. Mary's afterwards."

"And who was this stranger?"

"George Glen he called himself, and said he had been quartermaster with Adam Mayle at Whydah. He was a squat, tarry man, of Adam's age or thereabouts, and the pair of them walked through the gates and crossed the fields over to the street of Hugh Town. I made haste to join Helen," Clutterbuck continued, and explained his words with an unnecessary confusion. "I mean, I would not have it appear that she shared in the disgrace which had befallen Cullen Mayle. So I walked with her, and we followed Adam down the street to the Customs House, where it seemed every inhabitant was loitering, and where Cullen sat, with his hat cocked forward over his forehead to shield him from the sun, entirely at his ease.

"It was curious to observe the behaviour of the loiterers. Some affected not to see Cullen at all; some, but those chiefly maidens, protested that it was a great shame so fine a gentleman should be so barbarously used. The elders on the other hand answered that he had come over late to his deserts, while a few, with a ludicrous pretence of unconsciousness, bowed and smiled at him as though it was the most natural thing in the world for a man in a laced coat to take the air in the stocks of a Sunday morning.

"Into the midst of this group marched Adam Mayle, and came to a halt before his son. He had composed his face to an unexceptionable gravity, and as he prodded thoughtfully with his stick at the sole of Cullen's shoe,

"'This is the first time,' he said, 'that ever I saw a pair of silk stockings in the stocks.'

"'One lives and learns,' replied Cullen, indifferently; and the old man lifted his nose into the air and said dreamily:

"'There is a ducking-chair, is there not, at the pier head?' and so walked on to the steps where his boat was moored. He went down into it with Mr. Glen, and the two men set about hoisting the sail. I was still standing on the pier with Helen.

"'You will come too?' she said with a sort of appeal. 'I do not know what may happen when Cullen is set free and comes back. I should be very glad if you would come.'"

Lieutenant Clutterbuck broke off his story and walked uneasily once or twice across the room as though he was troubled even now with the recollection of her appeal and of how she looked when she made it.

"So I went," he continued suddenly, and with a burst of frankness. "You see, Steve, she and I were very good friends; I never saw anything but welcome in her eyes when I crossed over to Tresco, and the kindliness of her voice had a warmth, and at times a tenderness, which I hoped meant more than friendship. Indeed, I would have staked my life she was ignorant of duplicity; and with Cullen she seemed always at some pains to conceal a repugnance. Well, I was young, I suppose; I saw with the eyes of youth, which see everything out of its due proportion. I crossed to Tresco, and while we were seated at dinner, about two hours later, Cullen Mayle strolled in and took his chair. Dick Parmiter had waited for him at St. Mary's until such time as he was set free, and had brought him across the Road.

"I cannot deny but what Cullen Mayle bore himself very suitably for the greater part of the time we were at table. Adam's blatant jests were enough to set any man's teeth on edge, yet Cullen made as though he did not hear a word of them, and talked politely upon indifferent topics to us and Mr. Glen. Adam, however, was not to be silenced that way. His banter became coarse and vindictive; for one thing he had drunk a deal of liquor, and for another he was exasperated that he could not provoke his son. I forget what particular joke he roared out from the head of the table, but I saw Cullen stretch his arm out over the cloth.

"'I see what is amiss,' he said, wearily, and took away the brandy bottle from his father's elbow. He went to the window, and opening it, emptied the bottle on to the grass beneath the sill. Then he came back to his seat and said suavely to Mr. Glen: 'My father cannot get the better of his old habits; he is drunk very early on Sundays—an unregenerate old put of a fellow as ever I came across.'

"The quarrel followed close upon the heels of that sentence, and occupied the afternoon and was renewed at supper. Adam very violent and blustering; Cullen very cool and composed, and only betraying his passion by the whiteness of his face. He used no oaths; he sat staring at his father with his dark sleepy eyes, and languidly accused him of every crime in the Newgate Calendar, with a great deal of detail as to time and place, and adding any horrible detail which came into his mind. The old man was routed at the last. About the middle of supper he got up from his chair, and going up the stairs shut himself into a room which he had fitted up as a cabin, and where he was used to sit of an evening.

"We were all, as you may guess, inexpressibly relieved when Adam left the parlour, for here it seemed was the quarrel ended. We counted, however, without Cullen. He looked for a moment or two at his father's empty chair, and stood up in his turn.

"'Here's an old rogue for you,' he said in a gentle voice. 'He has no more manners than a nasty pig. I'll teach him some,' and he followed his father up the stairs and into the cabin above. What was said between them we never heard, but we gathered at the foot of the stairs in the hall and listened to their voices. The old man bellowed as though he was in pain, and shook the windows with his noise; Cullen's voice came to us only as a smooth, continuous murmur. For half an hour perhaps we stood thus in the hall—interference would have only made matters worse—and I own that this half hour was not wholly unpleasant to me. Helen, in a word, was afraid, and more than once her hand was laid upon my coat-sleeve, and, touching it, ceased to tremble. She turned to me, it seemed, in that half hour of fear; I was fool enough to think it.

"At length we heard a door opening. Cullen negligently came down the stairs; Adam rushed out after him as far as the head of the stairs, where he stopped.

"'Open the door, one of you!' he bawled. 'Kick him out, Clutterbuck, and we'll see what damned muck-heap his fine manners will lead him to.'

"The outcry brought the servants scurrying into the hall. Adam repeated his order and one of the servants threw open the door.

"'Will you fetch me my boots?' said Cullen, and sitting down in a chair he kicked off his shoes. Then he pulled on his boots deliberately, stood up and felt in his pockets. From one pocket he drew out five guineas, from a second two, from a third four. These eleven guineas he held in his open hand.

"'They belong to you, I think,' he said, softly, poising them in his palm; and before any one could move a step or indeed guess at his intention, he raised his arm and flung them with all his force to where his father stood at the head of the stairs. Two of the guineas cut the old man in the forehead, and the blood ran down his face; the rest sparkled and clattered against the panels behind his head, whence they fell on to the stairs and rolled one by one down into the hall. No one spoke; no one moved. The brutal violence of the action for the moment paralysed every one; even Adam stood shaking at the stair head with his wits wandering. One by one the guineas rolled down the staircase, leaping from step to step, rattling as they leaped; and for a long time it seemed, one whirred and sang in a corner as it span round and settled down upon the boards; and when the coin had ceased to spin, still no one moved, no one spoke. A murmur of waves breaking lazily upon the sand, a breath of air stirring a shrub in the garden, the infinitesimal trumpeting of a gnat, came through the window, bringing as it were tales of things which lived into a room of statues.

"Cullen himself was the first to break the enchantment. He took his watch from his fob and holding it by the ribbon twirled it backwards and forwards. It was a big silver watch, and as he twirled it this way and that, it caught the light, seemed to throw out little sparks of fire, and flashed with a dazzling brightness. The eyes of the company were caught by it; they watched it with a keen attention, not knowing why they watched it; they watched it as it shone and glittered in its revolutions, almost with a sense of expectation, as though something of great consequence was to happen from the twirling of that watch.

"'This, too, is yours,' said Cullen, 'but it was no doubt some dead sailorman's before you stole it;' and ceasing to twirl the watch he held it steady by the ribbon. Then he looked round the hall and saw Helen staring at the watch with a queer intentness. I remember that her hand was at that moment resting upon my sleeve, and I felt it grow more rigid. I looked at her; her face was set, her eyes fixed upon Cullen and his glittering watch. I spoke to her; she did not answer, she did not hear."

Clutterbuck interrupted his story and sat moodily lost in his recollections, and when he resumed it was with great bitterness.

"I think," he continued, "that when Cullen spoke, he spoke with no other end than to provoke his father yet more. You must know that the old man had just one tender spot in his heart. Cullen could have no other aim but to set his heel on that.

"'I will come back for you, Helen,' he said, bending his eyes upon her and making as if there was much love between them; and to everybody's surprise Helen lifted her eyes slowly from the watch until they met Cullen's, and kept them there. She did not answer him in words, there was no need she should, every line of her body expressed obedience.

"Even Cullen was puzzled by her demeanour. Boy and girl, maid and youth, they had lived side by side in the house with indifference upon his part and all the appearance of aversion upon hers. Yet here was she subdued in an instant at the prospect of his departure! It seemed that the mere thought that Cullen was henceforth an outcast tore her secret live and warm from her heart.

Cullen was plainly puzzled, as I say, but he was not the man to miss an advantage in the gratification of his malice. He shot one triumphant look at his father and spoke again to Helen.

"'You will wait for me?'

"Her eyes never wavered from his.

"'Yes!' she answered.

"It was a humiliating moment for me as you may imagine. It must have been more humiliating for Adam. With a hand upon the rail he lumbered heavily down a couple of the stairs.

"'No!' he cried, with a dreadful oath and in a voice which was strangely moved.

"'But I say yes,' said Cullen, very quietly. The smile had gone from his face; a new excitement kindled it. He was pitting his will against his father's. I saw him suddenly draw himself erect. 'Or, better still, you shall come with me now,' he cried. He reached out his arm straight from the shoulder towards her.

"'Come! Come with me now.'

" His voice rang out dominant like the clang of a trumpet, and to the consternation of us all, Helen crossed the floor towards him. I tried to detain her. ' Helen,' I cried, ' you do not know what you are doing. He will drag you into the gutter.'

"' Lieutenant Clutterbuck,' said Cullen, 'you are very red in the face. You cannot expect she will listen to you, for you do not look well when you are red in the face.'

" I paid no heed to his gibes.

"' Helen,' I cried, again. She paid no more heed to my prayers. ' What will you do ? Where will you go ? ' I asked.

"'We shall go to London,' answered Cullen, ' where we shall do very well, and further to the best of our means Lieutenant Clutterbuck's advancement.'

" Humiliation and grief had overset my judgment or I should not have argued at this moment with Cullen Mayle. I flung out at him hotly, and like a boy.

"'When you are doing very well in London, Cullen Mayle, Lieutenant Clutterbuck will not be so far behind you.'

"'He will indeed be close upon my heels,' returned Cullen as pleasantly as possible, 'for most likely he will be carrying my valise.'

"With that he turned again to Helen, beckoned her to follow him, and strode towards the open door. She did follow him. Cullen was already in the doorway; in another second she would have crossed the threshold. But with a surprising agility Adam Mayle jumped down the stairs, ran across the hall, and caught the girl in his arms. She did not struggle to free herself, but she strained steadily towards Cullen. The old man's arms were strong, however.

"'Shut the door,' he cried, and I sprang forward and slammed it to.

"'Lock it! Bolt it!'

"Adam stood with his arms about the girl until the heavy bar swung down across the door and dropped into its socket with a clang. Now do you understand why I will not go down to Tresco? I can give you another reason if you are not content. When I spoke to Helen two days later, and taxed her with her passion for Cullen,—would you believe it?—she was deeply pained and hurt. She would not have it said that she had so much as thought of following Cullen's fortunes. She outfaced me as though I had been telling her fairy tales, and not what my own eyes saw. No, indeed, I will not go down to Tresco! I am not the traveller who has ridden into your wood upon the Great West Road."

Lieutenant Clutterbuck took up his hat when he had finished his story,

"The girl, besides, is not worth a thought," said he.

"I am not thinking of her," said I. Of Lieutenant Clutterbuck, of myself, above all of Dick Parmiter, I was thinking, but not at all of Helen Mayle. I drew the map towards me. Clutterbuck stopped at the door, came back and again leaned over my shoulder.

"Has your traveller come out from that wood?" he asked.

"No," I answered.

"It is an allegory," said he. "The man who rides down on this business to the West will, in very truth, enter into a wood from which he will not get free."

CHAPTER V

THE ADVENTURE IN THE WOOD

A LOUD roll of drums beneath my windows, the inspiriting music of trumpets, the lively measured stamp of feet. The troops with General Amherst at their head were marching down St. James's Street on their way to embark for Canada, and the tune to which they marched sang in my head that day as I rode out of London. The beat of my horse's hoofs kept time to it, and at Brentford a girl singing in a garden of apple-trees threw me a snatch of a song to fit to it.

She sang, and I caught the words up as I rode past. The sparkle of summer was in the air, and an Indian summer, if you will, at my heart. I slept that night at Hartley Row, and the next at Down House, and the third at a little inn some miles beyond Dorchester. A brook danced at the foot of the house, and sang me to sleep with the song I had heard at Brentford, and, as I lay in bed, I could see out of my window the starlight and the quiet fields white with a frost of dew and thickets of trees very black and still; and towards sunset upon the fourth day, I suddenly reined in my horse to one side and sat stone-still. To my left, the road ran straight and level for a long way, and nowhere upon it was there a living thing; on each side stretched fields and no one moved in them, and no house was visible. That way I had come, and I had remarked upon the loneliness. To my right, the road ran forward into a thick wood, and vanished beneath a roof of overhanging boughs. It was the aspect of that wood which took my breath away, and it surprised me because it was familiar. There was a milestone which I recognised just where the first tree overhung the road; there was a white gate in the hedge some twenty paces this side of the milestone. I knew that too. Just behind where I sat there should be three tall poplars ranged in a line like sentinels, the wood's outposts; I turned, and in the field behind me, the poplars reached up against the sky. I had no doubt they would be there, yet the sight of them fairly startled me. I had seen them—yes, but never in my life had I ridden along this road before. I had seen them only on the map in my lodging at St. James's Street.

The sun dropped down behind the trees, and the earth turned grey. I sat there in the saddle with I know not what superstitious fancies upon me. I could not but remember that the traveller had ridden into the wood, and had not ridden out and down the open bank of grass upon the other side. "What if his horse has stumbled?" Clutterbuck had asked. "What if he is lying at the roadside under the trees?" I could see that picture very clearly, and at last, very clearly too, the rider's face. I looked backwards down the road with an instinctive hope that some other traveller might be riding my way in whose company I might go along. But the long level slip of white was empty. All the warmth seemed to have gone from the world with the dropping of the sun. A sad chill twilight crept over the lonely fields. A shiver caught and shook me; I gathered up the reins and rode slowly among the trees, where already it was night.

I rode at first in the centre of the highway, and found the clatter of my horse's hoofs a very companionable sound. But in a little the clatter seemed too loud, it was too clear a warning of my approach, it seemed to me in some way a provocation of danger. I drew to one side of the road

THE ADVENTURE IN THE WOOD

where the leaves had drifted and made a carpet whereon I rode without noise. But now the silence seemed too eerie—I heard, and started at, the snapping of every twig. I strained my ears to catch the noise of creeping footfalls, and I was about to guide my horse back to the middle of the road, when I turned a corner suddenly, and saw in front of me in a space where the forest receded and let the sky through, lights gleaming in a window.

I set spurs to the horse and galloped up to the door. The house was an inn; the landlord was already at the threshold, and in a very short while I was laughing at my fears over my supper in the parlour.

"Am I your only guest to-night?" I asked.

"There is one other, sir," returned the landlord as he served me, and as he spoke I heard a footstep in the passage. The door was pushed open, and a young man politely bowed to me in the entrance.

"You have a very pretty piece of horseflesh, sir," said he, as he came into the room. "I took the liberty of looking it over a minute ago in the stables."

"It is not bad," said I. There was never a

man in the world who did not relish praise of his horse, and I warmed to my new acquaintance. "We are both, it seems, sleeping here to-night, and likely enough we are travelling the same road to-morrow."

The young man shook his head.

"I could wish indeed," said he, "that we might be fellow-travellers, but though it may well be we follow the same road, we do not, alas, travel in the same way," and he showed me his boots which were thickly covered with dust. "My horse fell some half-a-dozen miles from here and snapped a leg. I must needs walk to-morrow so far as where I trust to procure another—that is to say," he continued, "if I do not have to keep my bed, for I have taken a devilish chill this evening," and drawing up his chair to the empty fireplace, he crouched over an imaginary fire and shivered.

Now since he sat in this attitude, I could not but notice his boots, and I fell to wondering what in the world he had done with his spurs. For he wore none, and since he had plainly not troubled to repair the disorder of his dress, it seemed strange that he should have gone to the pains of removing his spurs. However, I was soon diverted from this speculation by the distress

THE ADVENTURE IN THE WOOD 69

into which Mr. Featherstone's cold threw him. Featherstone was his name, as he was polite enough to tell me in the intervals of coughing, and I told him mine in return. At last his malady so increased that he called for the landlord, and bidding him light a great fire in his bedroom said he must needs go to bed

"I trust, however," he continued politely to me, "that you, Mr. Berkeley, will prove a Samaritan, and keep me company for a while. For I shall not sleep, upon my word I shall not sleep a wink," and he was so positive in his assurances that, though I was myself sufficiently tired, I thought it no more than kindness to fall in with his wishes.

Accordingly I followed him into his bedroom, where he lay in a great canopied bed, with a big fire blazing upon the hearth, and a bottle of rum with a couple of glasses upon a table at the bedside.

"It is an ague," said he, "which I caught upon the Gambia River, and from which I have ever since suffered many inconveniences;" he poured out the rum into the glasses, and wished me with great politeness all prosperity.

It was no doubt, also, because he had voyaged

on the Gambia River that he suffered no inconvenience from the heat of the room. But what with the hot August night, and the blazing fire, and the closed window, I became at once so drowsy that I could hardly keep my eyes open, and I wished him good-night.

"But you will not go," said he. "We are but this moment acquainted, and to-morrow we shall wave a farewell each to the other. Let us, Mr. Berkeley, make something of the meanwhile, I beg you."

I answered him that I did not wish to appear churlish, but that I should most certainly appear so if I fell asleep while we talked, which, in spite of myself, I was very likely to do.

"But I have a bottle of salts here," said he, with a laugh, as he reached out of bed and fumbled with his coat. "I have a bottle of salts here which will infallibly persuade you from any thought of sleep," and he drew out from the pocket of his coat a pack of cards. "Well, what do you say?" he continued, as I did not move.

"It is some while since I handled a card," said I slowly.

"A game of picquet," he suggested.

"It is a good game," said I.

THE ADVENTURE IN THE WOOD

He flipped the edges of the cards with his thumb. I drew nearer to the bed.

"Well, one game then," said I.

"To be sure," said he, shuffling the cards.

"And the stakes must be low."

"I hate a gambler myself."

He cut the cards. I sat down on the bedside and dealt them.

"It is your elder," said I.

He looked disconsolately at his hand.

"Upon my word," said he. "Deuce take me if I know what to discard. I have no hand for picquet at all, though as luck will have it I have very good putt cards."

I glanced through my hand.

"I have better putt cards than you," said I.

"It is not likely," he returned.

"I'll make a wager of it," I cried.

"Your horse," said he, leaning up on his elbow. He spoke a trifle too eagerly, he sprang up on his elbow a trifle too quickly. I looked again through my hand, and I laid the cards down on the counterpane.

"No," said I quietly. "It is very likely you are right: I have two treys and an ace, but you may have two treys and a deuce."

"Why, this is purely magical," he exclaimed, with the most natural burst of laughter imaginable. "Two treys and a deuce! Those are indeed the cards I hold."

He fell back again in the bed, and we played our single game of picquet. He won the game. Indeed, he could not but win it, for I paid no attention whatever to the cards which I held, or to how I should draw, or—and this perhaps was my most important omission—to how Mr. Featherstone shuffled and dealt. The truth is, I had suddenly become very curious about Mr. Featherstone. I had recalled his great politeness of manner. I remarked his face, which was of an almost girlish delicacy. I reflected that here was a man in a great hurry to travel by the same road as myself, and I remembered how I had learned that trick by which he had tried to outwit me of my horse. Even as it was I had all but fallen into the trap. I should most certainly have done so had not Lieutenant Clutterbuck once explained it to me on a particular occasion. I remembered that occasion very clearly as I sat on the bed playing this game of picquet by the light of a single candle, and I wondered whether I could fit Mr. Featherstone with another name.

"I am afraid," said he, "that this is a capote," as I played my last card.

"But the loss is trifling," said I, "and I have kept my horse."

"Very true," said he, whistling softly between his teeth. "You have kept your horse," and as I wished him good-night, he added, "you will be careful to shut the door behind you, won't you?"

But before the words were out of his mouth, he was seized with so violent a paroxysm of shivering that he could barely stammer out the end of the sentence.

"These infernal fevers," said he, with a groan.

"I notice, however," I returned, "that they are intermittent," and latching the door as he again requested me, I went off to my own room.

I could not but wonder what trickery the fire was intended to help, for until the last fit of the ague had seized him, he had given no sign of any sickness since he had brought out the cards. However, there was a more important question to occupy my mind. I had little doubt that Mr. Featherstone was Cullen Mayle: I had little doubt that he was hurrying as fast as he could to the Scillies, since he had received no answer to the message which he sent with the negro. But should I tell him of the men who watched for his coming, keeping their watches as at sea? On the one side their presence meant danger to Cullen Mayle, it could hardly mean anything else; and since it meant danger he should be warned of it.

On the other hand, the watchers might have tired of their watching and given it up as profitless. Besides I was by no means sure in what light Cullen himself was to be regarded. Was his return to Tresco, a prospect to be welcomed or deplored? Did he come as a friend to that distracted girl alone in the lonely house by the sand? I could not answer these questions. I knew Cullen to be a knave, I knew that the girl cared for him, and these two items made the sum of my knowledge. I turned over in my bed and fell asleep, thinking that my course might be clear to me in the morning.

And in the morning it was clear. I woke up with a mind made up. I had a horse; Cullen travelled on foot; since he had come so far on foot, it was not likely that he had the money to purchase a horse, for the story of the stumble and the broken leg I entirely disbelieved, and with the best of reasons. I had travelled myself along that road yesterday, and I had passed no disabled horse upon the way. I had therefore the advantage of Cullen. I would journey on without saying a word to him of my destination. I would on arriving take council with Dick Parmiter and Helen Mayle and seek to fathom the trouble. I should still have time to cross back to the mainland and hinder Cullen from attempting the passage.

Thus I planned to do, but the plan was never put to the test of action. For while I was still dressing, a loud hubbub and confusion filled the house. I opened my door. The noise came from the direction of Cullen's room. I hastily slipped on my coat and ran down the passage. I could hear Cullen's voice very loud above the rest, a woman or two protesting with a shrill indignation and the landlord trying to make all smooth, though what the bother was about I could not distinguish.

It seemed that the whole household was gathered in the room, though Mr. Featherstone still lay abed. The moment that I appeared in the doorway,

"Ah! here's a witness," he cried. "Mr. Berkeley, you were the last to leave me last night. You closed the door behind you? I was particular to ask you to close the door?"

"I remember that very well," said I, "for I was

wondering how in the world you could put up with the door closed and a blazing fire."

"There!" cried Featherstone turning to the landlord. "You hear? Mr. Berkeley is a gentleman beyond reproach. He shut the door behind him, and this morning I find it wide open and my breeches gone. There is a thief, sir, in your inn, and we travellers must go on our way without breeches. It is the most inconsiderate theft that ever I heard of."

"As for the breeches, sir," began the landlord.

"I don't care a button for them," cried Featherstone. "But there was money in the breeches' pockets. Fifteen guineas in gold, and a couple of bills on Mr. Nossiter, the banker at Exeter."

"The bills can be stopped," said the landlord. "We are but eighteen miles from Exeter."

"But how am I to travel those miles; do you expect me to walk there in my shirt tails. No, I stay here in bed until my breeches are found, and, burn me, if I don't eat up everything in the house," and immediately he began to roar out for food. "I will have chops at once, and there's a great sirloin of beef, and bring me a tankard of small ale."

Then he turned again to me, and said pathetically,

"It is not the breeches I mind, though to be sure I shall cut a ridiculous figure on the high-road; no, nor the money, though I have not a stiver left. But I woke up this morning in the sweetest good-humour, and here am I in a violent passion at nine o'clock in the morning, and my whole day spoilt. It is so discouraging," and he lay back upon the pillow as though he would have wept.

The landlord offered him his Sunday breeches. They were of red cloth, and a belted earl might wear them without shame.

"But not without discomfort," grumbled Mr. Featherstone, contemplating the landlord who was of a large figure. "They will hang about me in swathes like a petticoat."

"And as for the fifteen guineas," said I, "my purse is to that amount at your disposal."

"That is a very gentlemanly offer, Mr. Berkeley," said he, "from one stranger to another. But I have a horror of borrowing. I cannot accept your munificence. No, I will walk in my host's red cloth breeches as far as Rockbere, which to be sure is no more than twelve miles, quite penniless, but when I reach my friends, upon my word, I will make such a noise about this inn as will close its doors, strike me dead and stiff, if I don't."

His threat had its effect. The landlord, after the usual protestations that such an incident had never occurred before, that he had searched the house even to the servants' boxes, and that he could make neither head nor tail of the business, wound up his harangue with an offer of five guineas.

"It is all I have in the house, sir," said he, "and of course I shall charge you neither for food nor lodging."

"Of course not," said Mr. Featherstone indignantly. "Well, I must make the best of it, but oh! I woke up with so happy a disposition towards the world;" and dismissing the women he got up and dressed. The landlord fetched the five guineas and his red cloth breeches, which Featherstone drew on.

"Was ever a man so vilely travestied?" he said. "Sure, I shall be taken for a Hollander. That is hard for a person of some elegance," and he tied his cravat and went grumbling from the room.

"This is a great misfortune, sir, for me," said

THE ADVENTURE IN THE WOOD

my host. "I have lived honest all my days. There is no one in the house who would steal; on that I would stake my life. I can make nothing of it."

"Mr. Featherstone is quite recovered from his ague," said I slowly. I crossed over to the empty fireplace heaped with the white ashes of the logs which had blazed there the night before.

"The fire no doubt did him some benefit."

"That is precisely what I was thinking," said I, and I knelt down on the hearth-rug and poked amongst the ashes with the shovel. Suddenly, the landlord uttered an exclamation and threw up the window. I heard the clatter of a horse's hoofs upon the road. I got up from my knees and rushed to the window. As I leaned out Mr. Featherstone rode underneath and he rode my horse.

"Stop!" I shouted out.

"Mr. Berkeley," he cried, airily waving his hand as he rode by, "you may hold very good putt cards, but you haven't kept your horse."

"You damned thief!" I yelled, and he turned in his saddle and put out his tongue. It is, if you think of it, a form of repartee to which there is no reply. In any case I doubt if I could have made any reply which would have reached his ears. For he had set the horse to a gallop and was far down the road.

I went back to the hearth where the landlord joined me. We both knelt down and raked away the ashes.

"What's that?" said I, pointing to something blackened and scorched. The landlord picked it up.

"It is a piece of corduroy."

"And here's a bone button," said I. "The ague was a sham, the fire a device to rob you. He came here without a penny piece and burnt his breeches last night. He has robbed you, he has robbed me, and he will reach the Scilly Islands first. How far is it to Rockbere?"

"Twelve miles."

"I must walk those twelve miles?"

"Yes."

"Will I get a horse there?"

"It is doubtful."

"He has a day's start then at the least."

So after all, though the horse did not stumble, nor the rider lie quiet by the roadside, he did not ride out of the forest at a gallop, and down the green bank into the open space beyond.

CHAPTER VI

MY FIRST NIGHT UPON TRESCO

I WALKED that day into Rockbere, and taking the advice of the innkeeper with whom I lodged, I hired a hack and a guide from him the next morning and struck across country for the sea; for he assured me that I should most likely find a fishing smack at Topsham whose master would put me over to the Scillies, and that if the wind did but favour me I should reach the islands sooner that way than if I had the quickest horse under me that was ever foaled. It was of the greatest urgency that I should set foot on Tresco before Cullen Mayle. I had to risk something to achieve that object, and I risked the wind. It was in the northeast when I started from Rockbere and suited my purpose finely if it did but hold; so that I much regretted I was not already on the sea, and rode in a perpetual fear lest it should change its quarter. I came to Honiton Clyst that night, and to Topsham the next day, where I was fortunate enough to find a boat of some thirty tons and to come to an agreement with its master. He had his crew ready to his hand; he occupied the morning in provisioning the smack; and we stood out of the harbour in the evening, and with a steady wind on our quarter made a good run to the Start Point. Shortly after we passed the Start the wind veered round into the north, which did us no great harm, since these boats sail their best on a reach. We reached then with a soldier's breeze, as the saying is, out to the Eddystone Rock and the Lizard Point.

It was directly after we had sighted the Lizard that the wind began to fall light, and when we were just off the Point it failed us altogether. I remember that night as well as any other period in the course of these incidents. I was running a race with Cullen Mayle, and I was beginning to think that it was not after all only on account of his peril that it was needful for me to reach Tresco before he did. These last two days I had been entirely occupied with the stimulation of that race and the inspiriting companionship of the sea. The waves foaming away from the bows and bubbling and hissing under the lee of the boat, the flaws of wind blistering the surface of the water as they came off the land towards us, making visible their invisible approach; the responsive spring of the boat, like a horse under the touch of a spur—these mere commonplaces to my companions had for me an engrossing enchantment. But on that evening at the Lizard Point the sea lay under the sunset a smooth, heaving prism of colours; we could hear nothing but the groaning of the blocks, the creaking of the boom's collars against the masts; and the night came out from behind the land very peaceful and solemn, and solemnly the stars shone out in the sky. All the excitement of the last days died out of me. We swung up and down with the tide. Now the lights of Falmouth were visible to us at the bottom of the bay, now the Lizard obscured them from us. I was brought somehow to think of those last years of mine in London. They seemed very distant and strange to me in this clean air, and the pavement of St. James's Street, which I had daily trodden, became an unacceptable thing.

About two o'clock of the morning a broad moon rose out of the sea, and towards daybreak a little ruffling breeze sprang up, and we made a gentle progress across the bay towards Land's

End; but the breeze sank as the sun came up, and all that day we loitered, gaining a little ground now and then and losing it again with the turn of the tide. It was not until the fifth evening that we dropped anchor in the road between St. Mary's Island and Tresco.

I waited until it was quite dark, and was then quietly rowed ashore with my valise in the ship's dinghy. I landed on Tresco near to the harbour of New Grimsby. It was at New Grimsby that Dick Parmiter lived, Clutterbuck had told me, and the first thing I had to do was to find Dick Parmiter without arousing any attention.

Now on an island like Tresco, sparsely inhabited and with no commerce, the mere presence of a stranger would assuredly provoke comment. I walked, therefore, very warily towards the village. One house I saw with great windows all lighted up, and that I took to be the Palace Inn, where Adam Mayle and Cullen used to sit side by side on the settle and surprise the visitors by their unlikeness to one another. There was a small cluster of cottages about the inn with a lane straggling between, and further away, round the curve of the little bay, were two huts close to the sea.

It would be in one of these that Dick Parmiter

MY FIRST NIGHT UPON TRESCO   85

lived, and I crept towards them. There was no light whatever in the first of them, but the door stood open, and a woman and a man stood talking in the doorway. I lay down in the grass and crawled towards them, if by any chance I might hear what they said. For a while I could distinguish nothing of what they said, but at last the man cried in a clear voice, "Good-night, Mrs. Crudge," and walked off to the inn. The woman went in and closed the door. I was sure then that the next cottage was the one for which I searched. I walked to it; there was a light in the window and the sound of voices talking.

I hesitated whether to go in boldly and ask for Dick. But it would be known the next morning that a stranger had come for Dick; no doubt, too, Dick's journey to London was known, and the five men watching the house on Merchant's Point would be straightway upon the alert. Besides Dick might not have reached home. I walked round the hut unable to decide what I should do, and as I came to the back of it a light suddenly glowed in a tiny window there. I cautiously approached the window and looked through. Dick Parmiter was stripping off his jersey, and was alone.

I tapped on the window. Dick raised his head, and then put out the light, so that I could no longer see into the room; but in a moment the window was slowly lifted, and the boy's voice whispered:

"Is that you, Mr. Mayle?"

I drew a breath of relief. I was ahead of Cullen Mayle, though he had stolen my horse.

"No," said I; "but I have come on Cullen Mayle's business."

The boy leaned out of the window and peered into my face. But voices were raised in the room beyond this cupboard, and a woman's voice cried out, "Dick, Dick!"

"That's mother," said Dick to me. "Wait! I will come out to you."

He closed the window, and I lay down again in the grass, and waited there for perhaps an hour. A mist was coming up from the sea and thickening about the island; the starlight was obscured; wreaths of smoke, it seemed, came in puffs between myself and the house, and at last I heard the rustling of feet in the grass.

"Dick," said I in a whisper, and the lad came to me.

"I remember you," he said. "You were at

MY FIRST NIGHT UPON TRESCO 87

Lieutenant Clutterbuck's. Why have you come?"

"Upon my word," said I, "I should find it difficult to tell you."

Indeed, it would have taken me half the night to explain the motives which had conjoined to this end.

"And now that you are come, what is it you mean to do?"

"Dick," I returned, "you ask the most disconcerting questions. You tramp up to London with a wild story of a house watched——"

"You come as a friend, then," he broke in eagerly.

"As your friend, yes."

Dick sat silent for a moment.

"I think so," he said at length.

"And here's a trifle to assure you," I said. "Cullen Mayle is not very far behind me. You may expect him upon Tresco any morning."

Dick started to his feet.

"Are you sure of that? You do not know him. How are you sure?"

"Clutterbuck described him to me. I overtook him on the road, and stayed the same night with him at an inn. He robbed me and robbed the landlord. There was a trick at the cards, too. Not a doubt of it, Cullen Mayle is close on my heels. Are those five men still watching the house?"

"Yes. They are still upon Tresco. They lodge here and there with the fishermen, and make a pretence to burn kelp or to fish for their living; but their business is to watch the house, as you will see to-night. There are six of them now, not five."

He led me as he spoke towards the "Palace Inn," where a light still burned in the kitchen. The cottages about the inn, however, were by this time dark, and we could advance without risk of being seen. Dick stopped me under the shadow of a wall not ten yards from the inn. A red blind covered the lower part of the window, but above it I could see quite clearly into the kitchen.

"Give me a back," whispered Dick, who reached no higher than my shoulder. I bent down and Dick climbed on to my shoulders, whence he too could see the interior of the kitchen.

"That will go," said he in a little, and slid to the ground. "Can you see a picture on the wall?"

"Yes."

"And a man sitting under the picture—a squat, squabby man with white hair and small eyes very bright?"

"Yes."

"That is the sixth man. He came to Tresco while I was in London. I found him here when I came back two days ago. But I had seen him before. He had come to Tresco before. His name is George Glen."

"George Glen!" said I. "Wait a bit," and I took another look at the man in the kitchen. "He was quartermaster with Adam Mayle at Whydah, eh? He is the stranger you brought over to St. Mary's Church on the day when Cullen Mayle sat in the stocks."

"Yes," said Dick, and he asked me how I knew.

"Clutterbuck told me," I replied.

From the inn we walked some few yards along a lane until we were free of the cottages, and then leaving the path, mounted inland up a hill of gorse. Dick gave me on the way an account of his journey homewards and the difficulties he had surmounted. I paid only an indifferent attention to his story, for I was wholly occupied with George Glen's presence upon the island. Glen had come first of all to visit Adam Mayle, and was now watching for Cullen. What link was there between his two visits? I was inclined to think that George Glen was the clue to the whole mystery. In spite of my inattention, I gathered this much however from Dick. That tramp of his to London was well known throughout the islands. His mother had given him up for dead when he went away, and had thrashed him soundly when he returned, but the next day had made him out a great hero in her talk. She did not know why he went to London, for Dick had the discretion to hold his tongue upon that point.

So much Parmiter had told me when he suddenly stopped and listened. I could hear nothing, however much I strained my ears, and in a moment or two Dick began to move on. The mist was very thick about us—I could not see a yard beyond my nose; but we were now going down hill, so that I knew we had crossed the ridge of the island and were descending towards the harbour of New Grimsby and the house under Merchant's Rock.

We had descended for perhaps a couple of hundred yards; then Dick stopped again. He laid a hand upon my arm and dragged me down among the gorse, which was drenched with the fog.

MY FIRST NIGHT UPON TRESCO 91

"What is it?" said I.

"Hush," he whispered; and even as he whispered I saw a sort of brown radiance through the fog a long way to my left. The next instant a speck of clear light shone out in the heart of this radiance: it was the flame of a lantern, and it seemed miles away. I raised myself upon my elbows to watch it. Dick pulled my elbow from beneath me, and pressed me down flat in the grass; and it was fortunate that he did, for immediately the lantern loomed out of the fog not a dozen yards away. I heard it rattle as it swung, and the man who carried it tramped by so near to me that if I had stretched out my hand I could have caught him by the ankle and jerked him off his feet. It was the purest good fortune that he did not detect us, and we lay very still until the rustle of the footsteps had altogether died away.

"Is that one of them?" I asked.

"Yes; William Blads. He lodges with Mrs. Crudge next to our cottage."

We continued to descend through the gorse for another quarter of an hour or so until an extraordinary sound at our feet brought us both to an halt. It was the strangest melancholy screeching sound that ever I had heard: it was so harsh it pierced the ears; it was so wild and eerie that I could hardly believe a voice uttered it. It was like a shrill cry of pain uttered by some live thing that was hardly human. It startled me beyond words, and the more so because it rose out of the fog directly at our feet. Dick Parmiter trembled at my side.

"Quick," he whispered in a shaking voice; "let us go! Oh, let us go!"

But he could not move for all his moaning. His limbs shook as though he had the fever; terror chained him there to the ground. Had I not known the boy under other circumstances, I should have set him down for a coward.

I took a step forward. Dick caught hold of my arm and muttered something, but his voice so wavered and gasped I could not distinguish what he said. I shook his arm off, and again stepped forward for one, two, three paces. As I took the third pace the ground suddenly sloped, my feet slipped on the wet grass; I let go of my valise, and I fell to my full length upon my back, and slid. And the moment I began to slide my feet touched nothing. I caught at the grass, and the roots of it came away in my hands. I turned over on my face. Half my body was now hanging over the edge. I hung for a second by my waist, and as I felt my waist slipping, I struck out wildly upon each side with my arms. My right arm struck against a bush of gorse; I seized hold of it, and it bent, but it did not break. I lifted a knee carefully, set it on the edge, and so crawled up the slope again.

Dick was lying on his face peering down towards me.

"My God," said he, "I thought you had fallen;" and reaching out his hands, he caught both my arms as though he was afraid I should slip again. "Oh, quick," he said, "let us go!"

And again I heard the shrill screech rise up from that hollow into which I had so nearly fallen. It was repeated and repeated with a regular interval between—an interval long enough for Dick to reiterate his eager prayer.

"It has begun again," said I.

"It has never ceased since we first heard it," said Dick, and no doubt he spoke the truth; only I had been deaf to it from the moment my foot slipped until now. "Let us go," and picking up my valise he hurried me away, turning his head as he went, shuddering whenever he heard that cry.

"But it may be some one in distress—some one who needs help."

"No, no," he cried; "it is no one. I will tell you to-morrow."

We skirted the top of the hollow, and once more descended. The fog showed no sign of clearing, but Parmiter walked with an assured tread, and in a little time he began to recover his spirits.

"We are close to the house," said he.

"Dick, you are afraid of ghosts," said I; and while I spoke he uttered a cry and clung to my arm. A second later something brushed past my hand very quickly. I just saw it for an instant as it flitted past, and then the darkness swallowed it up.

Dick blurted out this fable: the souls of dead drowned sailormen kept nightly tryst on Castle Down.

"That was no spirit," said I. "Play the man, Dick. Did you ever meet a spirit that trod with the weight of a body?"

I could hear the sound of feet rustling the grass beneath us. Dick listened with his hand to his ear.

"The tread is very light," said he.

"That is because it is a woman who treads."

"No woman would be abroad here in this fog at this time," he protested.

"Nevertheless, it was a woman; for I saw her, and her dress brushed against my hand. It was a woman, and you cried out at her; so that if there is any one else upon the watch to-night, it is very likely we shall have him upon our heels."

That argument sobered him, and we went forward again without speaking to each other, and only halting now and again to listen. In a very short while we heard the sea booming upon the beach, and then Dick stepped forward yet more warily, feeling about with his hands.

"There should be a fence hereabouts," said he, and the next moment I fell over it with a great clatter. A loud whistle sounded from the beach—another whistle answered behind us, and I heard the sound of a man running up from the sand. We both crouched in the grass close by the palisade, and again the fog saved us. I heard some one beating about in the grass with a stick, but he did not come near us, and at last he turned back to the sea.

"You see," said Dick, "I told Lieutenant Clutterbuck the truth. The house is watched."

"Devil a doubt of it," said I. "Do you go forward and see if you can get in."

He came back to me in a little space of time, saying that the door was barred, and that he could see no light through any chink. He had stolen all round the house; he had rapped gently here and there at a window, but there was no one waking.

"And what are we to do now?" said he. "If I make a clatter and rouse the house, we shall rouse Cullen's enemies, too."

"It would not be wise to put them on the alert, the more particularly since Cullen Mayle may be here to-morrow. I will go back to the 'Palace' Inn, sleep the night there, and come over here boldly in the morning." And I got up and shouldered my valise again. But Dick stopped me.

"I have a better plan than that," said he, "for George Glen is staying at the 'Palace' Inn. What if you slept in the house here to-night! I can come over early to-morrow and tell Miss Helen who you are, and why you have come."

"But how am I to get into the house, without you rouse the household?"

"There is a window. It is the window of Cullen Mayle's room. You could get through it with my help."

MY FIRST NIGHT UPON TRESCO

It seemed in many ways the best plan that could be thought of, but certain words of Clutterbuck's that my meddling at all in the matter would be nothing but an impertinence came back very forcibly to me. But I heard Dick Parmiter speaking, and the thought slipped instantly from my mind.

"I helped Cullen Mayle through the window, the night his father drove him from the house," said he, "and——"

"What's that you say?" I asked eagerly. "The night that Cullen Mayle was driven from the house, he climbed back into his room!"

"Yes!"

"Tell me about it, and be quick!" said I. I had my own reason for urging him, and I listened with all my attention to every word he spoke. He told me the sequel of the story which Clutterbuck had related in my lodging at St. James's Street.

"I was waiting for him outside here on the beach," said he; "and when the door was closed behind him, he came straight towards me. 'And where am I to sleep to-night, Dick?' said he. I told him that he could have my bed over at New Grimsby, but he refused it. 'I'm damned if I sleep in a rat-hole,' he said, 'when by putting my pride in my pocket I can sleep in my own bed; and with my help he clambered on to an outhouse, and so back into his own room."

"When did he leave the island, then?" I asked. "The next morning? But no one saw him go?"

"No," answered Dick. "I sailed him across the same night. About three o'clock of the morning he came and tapped softly upon my window, just as you did to-night. It was that which made me think you were Cullen come back. He bade me slip out to him without any noise, and together we carried my father's skiff down to the water. I sailed him across to St. Mary's. He made me swear never to tell a word of his climbing back into his room."

"Oh, he made you swear that?"

"Yes, he said he would rip my heart out if I broke my oath. Well, I've kept it till to-night. No one knows but you. I got back to Tresco before my father had stirred."

"And Cullen?"

"A barque put out from St. Mary's to Cornwall with the first of the ebb in the morning. I suppose he persuaded the captain to take him."

MY FIRST NIGHT UPON TRESCO 99

Parmiter's story set me thinking, and I climbed over the palisade after him without further objection. He came to a wall of planks; Dick set himself firmly against it and bent his shoulders.

"This is an outhouse," said he. "From my shoulders you can reach the roof. From the roof you can reach the window. You can force the catch of the window with a knife."

"It will be an awkward business," said I doubtfully, "if I wake the house."

"There is no fear of that," answered Dick. "With any other window I would not say no. The other rooms are separated only by a thin panelling of wood, and at one end of the house you can almost hear a mouse scamper at the other. Mr. Cullen's room, however, is a room built on, its inner wall is the outer wall of the house, it is the one room where you could talk secrets and run no risk of being overheard."

"Very well," said I slowly, for this speech too set me thinking. "I will risk it. Come over early to-morrow, Dick. I shall cut an awkward figure without you do," and getting on to his shoulder, I clambered up on to the roof of the outhouse. He handed my valise to me; I pushed back the catch of the window with the blade of my knife, lifted it, threw my leg over the sill and silently drew myself into the room. The room was very dark, but my eyes were now accustomed to the gloom. I could dimly discern a great four-poster bed. I shut the window without noise, set my valise in a corner, drew off my boots and lay down upon the bed.

CHAPTER VII

TELLS OF AN EXTRAORDINARY INCIDENT IN CULLEN MAYLE'S BEDROOM

I WAS very tired, but in spite of my fatigue it was some while before I fell asleep. Parmiter had thrown a new light upon the business tonight, and by the help of that light I arrayed afresh my scanty knowledge. The strangeness of my position, besides, kept me in some excitement. Here was I quietly abed in a house where I knew no one; Clutterbuck might well talk about impertinence, and I could not but wonder what in the world I should find to say if Dick was late in the morning. Finally, there was the adventure of that night. I felt myself again slipping down the wet grass and dangling over the precipice. I heard again that unearthly screeching which had so frightened Dick and perplexed me, It perplexed me still. I could not for a moment entertain Dick's supposition of a spirit. This was the middle of the eighteenth century, you will understand, and I had come fresh from London. Ghosts and bogies might do very well for the island of Tresco, but Mr. Berkeley was not to be terrified with any such old-wives' stories, and so Mr. Berkeley fell asleep.

At what precise hour the thing happened I do not know. The room was so dark that I could not have read my watch, even if I had looked at it, which I did not think to do. But at some time during that night I woke up quite suddenly with a clear sense that I had been waked up.

I sat up in my bed with my heart beating very quick; and then with as a little noise as I could I gathered myself up in the shadow of the bed-hangings, at the head. The fog was still thick about the house, so that hardly a glimmer of light came from the window. But there was some one in the room I knew, for I could hear a rustle as of stealthy movements. And then straight in front of me between the two posts of the bed-foot, I saw something white that wavered and swayed this way and that. Only an hour or so before I had been boasting to myself that I was London-bred and lived in the middle of the eighteenth century. But none the less my hair stirred upon my head, and all the moisture dried up in my throat as

AN EXTRAORDINARY INCIDENT

I stared at that dim white thing wavering and swaying between the bed-posts. It was taller than any human being that I had seen. I remembered the weird screeching sound which I had heard in the hollow; I think that in my heart I begged Dick Parmiter's pardon for laughing at his fears; I know that I crouched back among the hangings and shuddered till the bed shook and shook again. And then it made a sound, and all the blood in my veins stood still. I thought that my heart would stop or my brain burst. For the sound was neither a screech like that which rose from the hollow, nor a groan, nor any ghostly noise. It was purely human, it was a kecking sound in the throat, such as one makes who gasps for breath. The white thing was a live thing of flesh and blood.

I sprang up on the bed and jumped to the foot of it. It was very dark in the room, but through the darkness, I could see, on a level with my face, the face of a woman. Her eyes were open and they stared into mine. I could see the whites of them; our heads were so near they almost touched.

Even then I did not understand. I wondered what it was on which she stood. I noticed a streak of white which ran straight up towards the ceiling from behind her head, and I wondered what that was. And then suddenly her body swung against my legs. She was standing on nothing whatever! Again the queer gasping coughing noise broke from her lips, and at last I understood it. It was a gasp of a woman strangling to death. That white stiff streak above her head—I knew what it was too. I caught her by the waist and lifted her up till her weight rested upon m arm. With the other arm I felt about her neck. A thick soft scarf—silk it seemed to the touch—was knotted tightly round it, and the end of the scarf ran up to the cross-beam above the bed-posts. The scarf was the streak of white.

I fumbled at the knot with my fingers. It was a slip knot, and now that no weight kept it taut, it loosened easily. I slipped the noose back over her head and left it dangling. The woman I laid down upon the bed, where she lay choking and moaning.

I flung up the window and the cold fog poured into the room. I had no candle to light and nothing wherewith to light it. But I remembered that my foot had knocked against a chair to the right of the window, as I climbed into the room.

I groped for the chair and set it to face the open night. Then I carried the woman to the window and placed her in the chair, and supported her so that she might not fall. Outside I could hear the surf booming upon the sand almost within arm's reach, and the air was brisk with the salt of the sea.

Such light as there was, glimmered upon the woman's face. I saw that she was young, little more than a girl indeed, with hair and eyes of an extreme blackness. She was of a slight figure as I knew from the ease with which I carried her, but tall. I could not doubt who it was, for one thing the white dress she wore was of some fine soft fabric, and even in that light it was easy to see that she was beautiful.

I held her thus with the cold salt air blowing upon her face, and in a little, she began to recover. She moved her hands upon her lap, and finally lifted one and held her throat with it.

"Very likely there will be some water in the room," said I. "If you are safe, if you will not fall, I will look for it."

"Thank you," she murmured.

My presence occasioned her no surprise and this I thought was no more than natural at the moment. I took my arm from her waist and groped about the room for the water-jug. I found it at last and a glass beside it. These I carried back to the window.

The girl was still seated on the chair, but she had changed her attitude. She had leaned her arms upon the sill and her head upon her arms. I poured out the water from the jug into the tumbler. She did not raise her head. I spoke to her. She did not answer me. A horrible fear turned me cold. I knelt down by her side, and setting down the water gently lifted her head. She did not resist but sank back with a natural movement into my arms. Her eyes were closed, but she was breathing. I could feel her breath upon my cheek and it came steadily and regular. I cannot describe my astonishment; she was in a deep sleep.

I pondered for a moment what I should do! Should I wake the household? Should I explain what had happened and my presence in the house? For Helen Mayle's sake I must not do that, since Helen Mayle it surely was whom I held in my arms.

I propped her securely in the chair, then crossed the room, opened the door and listened. The house was very still; so far no one had been disturbed. A long narrow passage stretched in front of me, with doors upon either side. Remembering what Dick Parmiter had told me, I mean that every sound reverberated through the house, I crept down the landing on tip-toe. I had only my stockings upon my feet and I crept forward so carefully that I could not hear my own footfalls.

I had taken some twenty paces when the passage opened out to my right. I put out my hand and touched a balustrade. A few yards farther on the balustrade ceased; there was an empty space which I took to be the beginning of the stairs, and beyond the empty space the passage closed in again.

I crept forward, and at last at the far end of the house and on the left hand of the passage I came to that for which I searched, and which I barely hoped to find—an open door. I held my breath and listened in the doorway, but there was no sound of any one breathing, so I stepped into the room.

The fog was less dense, it hung outside the window a thin white mist and behind that mist the day was breaking. I looked round the room. It was a large bedroom, and the bed had not been slept in. A glance at the toilette with its dainty knick-knacks of silver proved to me that it was a woman's bedroom. It had two big windows looking out towards the sea, and as I stood in the dim grey light, I wondered whether it was from one of those windows that Adam Mayle had looked years before, and seen the brigantine breaking up upon the Golden Ball Reef. But the light was broadening with the passage of every minute. With the same caution which I had observed before I stole back on tip-toe to Cullen Mayle's room. Helen Mayle was still asleep, and she had not moved from her posture. I raised her in my arms, and still she did not wake. I carried her down the passage, through the open door and laid her on the bed. There was a coverlet folded at the end of the bed and I spread it over her. She nestled down beneath it and her lips smiled very prettily, and she uttered a little purring murmur of content; but this she did in her sleep. She slept with the untroubled sleep of a child. Her face was pale, but that I took to be its natural complexion. Her long black eyelashes rested upon her cheeks. There was no hint of any trouble in her expression, no trace of any passionate despair. I could hardly believe that this was the girl who had sought to hang

AN EXTRAORDINARY INCIDENT

herself, whom I had seen struggling for her breath.

Yet there was no doubt possible. She had come into the empty room—empty as she thought, and empty it would have been, had not a fisher-boy burst one night into Lieutenant Clutterbuck's lodging off the Strand—when every one slept, and there she had deliberately stood upon the bed, fastened her noose to the cross-bar and sprang off. There was no doubt possible. It was her spring from the bed which had waked me up, and as I returned to Cullen's room, I saw the silk noose still hanging from the beam.

CHAPTER VIII

HELEN MAYLE

A LOUD rapping on the door roused me. The mist had cleared away, and out of the open window I could see a long sunlit slope of gorse all yellow and purple stretching upwards, and over the slope a great space of blue sky whereon the clouds sailed like racing boats in a strong breeze. The door was thrust open and Dick Parmiter entered.

"You keep London hours, sir," said he, standing at the foot of the bed, and he happened to raise his eyes. "What's that?" he asked.

That was the silk scarf still dangling from the cross-bar, and the sight of it brought back to me in a flash my adventure of the night. With the clear sunlight filling the room and the bright wind chasing the clouds over the sky, I could hardly believe that it had really occurred. But the silk scarf hung between the posts.

"My God," I cried out. "What if I had never waked up!"

There would have been the sunlight and the wind in the sky as now, but, facing me, no longer swaying, but still, inert, horrible, I should have seen—and I clapped my hands over my face, so distinct was this unspeakable vision to me, and cried out again: "What if I had not waked up!"

"You have not waked up very early," said Dick, looking at me curiously, and recovering my self-possession I hasten to explain.

"I have had dreams, Dick. The strange room! I am barely awake yet."

It appeared that I was not the only one to keep London hours that morning. It was close upon mid-day and Dick had not waked me before, because he had not before had speech with the mistress of the house. Helen Mayle had risen late. But she knew now of my presence in the house and what had brought me, and was waiting to offer me her thanks.

In spite of this news that she was waiting, I made my toilette very slowly. It would be the most awkward, embarrassing meeting imaginable. How could one bow and smile and exchange the trivial courtesies with a girl whom one had saved from that silk noose some eight hours before? With what countenance would she greet me? Would she resent my interference? Dick, however, had plainly noticed nothing unusual in her demeanour; I consoled myself with that reflection. He noticed, however, something unusual here in my room, for as I tied my cravat before the mirror I saw that he was curiously looking at the silk scarf.

"Perhaps you have seen it before," said I without turning round. Dick started, then he coloured.

"I was wondering why it hung there," said he.

"It *is* curious," said I calmly, and I stood upon the bed and with some trouble, for the knots were stiff, I took it down and thrust it into the pocket of my coat.

"It is yours?" cried Dick.

"One silk scarf is very like another," said I, and he coloured again and was silent. His silence was fortunate, since if he had asked to what end I had hung it above my bed, I should have been hard put to it for an answer.

"I am ready," said I, and we walked along the passage to the balustrade, and the head of the stairs where I had crept on tiptoe during the night.

I noticed certain marks, a few dents, a few scratches on the panels of the wall at the head of the stairs, and I was glad to notice them, for they reminded me of the business upon which I had come and of certain conjectures which Dick had suggested to my mind. It was at the head of the stairs that Adam Mayle had stood when he drove out his son. The marks no doubt were the marks of that handful of guineas which Cullen had flung to splatter and sparkle against the wall behind his father's head. I was glad to notice them, as I say, for the tragical incident in which I had borne a share that night had driven Cullen Mayle's predicament entirely from my thoughts.

I saw the flutter of a dress at the foot of the stairs, and a face looked up to mine. It was the face which I had seen on a level with mine in the black gloom of the night, and as I saw it now in the clear light of day, I stopped amazed. It wore no expression of embarrassment, no plea for silence. She met me with a grateful welcome in her eyes as for one who had come unexpectedly to do her a service, and perhaps a hint of curiosity as to why I should have come at all.

8

"Dick has told me of you," she said, as she held out her hand. "You are very kind. Until this morning I did not even know the reason of Dick's journey to London. I was not aware that he had paid a visit to Lieutenant Clutterbuck."

There was a trifle of awkwardness in her voice as she pronounced his name. I could not help feeling and no doubt expressing some awkwardness as I heard it. Lieutenant Clutterbuck had not hesitated to accuse her of duplicity; I at all events could not but acknowledge that she was excellently versed in the woman's arts of concealment. There was thus a moment's silence before I answered.

"You will accept me I hope as Lieutenant Clutterbuck's proxy."

"We had no right," she returned, "to expect any service from Lieutenant Clutterbuck, much less from——" and she hesitated and stopped abruptly.

"From a stranger you would have said," I added.

"We shall count you a stranger no longer," she said, with a frank smile, and that I might not be outdone in politeness, I said:

"If Dick had lacked discretion and told you all

that he might have told, you would understand that the obligation is upon my side. For whereas I do not know that I can render you any service whatever, I do know that already you have rendered me a great one."

"That is very prettily said," she returned, as she walked into the parlour.

"Truth at times," I answered lightly as I followed her, "can be as pretty as the most ingenious lie."

So that first awkward meeting was past. I took my cue from her reticence, but without her success. I could not imitate her complete unconsciousness. It seemed she had no troubles. She sat at the table in a flow of the highest spirits. Smiles came readily to her lips, and her eyes laughed in unison. She was pale and the pallor was the more marked on account of her dark hair and eyes, but the blood came and went in her cheeks, and gave to her an infinite variety of expression. I could hardly believe that this voice which was now lively with contentment was the voice which had uttered that kecking sound in the night, or that the eyes which now sparkled and flashed were the eyes which had stared at me through the gloom. No doubt I looked at her with more curiosity than was convenient; at all events she said, with a laugh:

"I would give much to know what picture Dick painted of me, for if I may judge from your looks, Mr. Berkeley, the likeness is very unlike to the original."

I felt my cheeks grow hot, and cast about for a reason to excuse my curiosity. Her own words suggested the reason.

"Dick told me," I said, "of a woman in great distress and perplexity, whose house was watched, who dreaded why it was watched——"

"And you find a woman on the top of her spirits," she broke in, and was silent for a little, looking at the cloth. "And very likely," she continued slowly, "you are disposed to think that you have been misled and persuaded hither for no more than a trivial purpose."

"No," I protested. "No such thought occurred to me," and in my anxiety to free myself from the suspicion of this imputation I broke through that compact of silence upon which we seemed silently to have agreed. "I have no reason for pride, God knows, but indeed, Madam, I am not so utterly despicable as to regret that I came to Tresco and crept into your house last night. Already,—suppose there was nothing more for me to do but to wish you a good-morning and betake myself back to town—already I have every reason to be glad that I came, for if I had not come——" and I stopped.

Helen Mayle listened to me with some surprise of manner at the earnestness with which I spoke and when I stopped so abruptly, she blushed and her eyes again sought the table.

"Yes," she said quietly, "Mr. Berkeley, you have guessed the reason of my good spirits. If you had not come, a woman in great distress and perplexity would be wandering restlessly about the house, as she did yesterday."

Her eyes were still fixed upon the table, or she must have remarked my astonishment and the pretence would at once and for all have been torn away from between us. I leaned back in my chair; it was as much as I could do to stifle an exclamation. If I had not come, a woman's spirit might be wandering to-day restlessly from room to room, but the woman—I had the silk scarf in my coat-pocket to assure me she would not.

"The distress and perplexity," she continued, "are not done with, but to-day a hand has been stretched to me out of the dark, and I must think, to some good end. It could not be otherwise," and she lifted her eyes to mine. I did not doubt their sincerity. "And—shall I tell you?" she continued with a frank smile. "I am glad, though I hardly know why—I am glad that the man who stretched out his hand was quite unknown to me and himself knew nothing of me, and had not so much as seen my face. He helps a woman, not *one* woman. I am more grateful for that, I take it to be of good augury." And she held her hand to me.

I took the hand; I was tempted to let her remain in her misapprehension. But sooner or later she would learn the truth, and it seemed to me best that she should learn something of it from me.

"Madam," I said, "I should account myself happy if I could honestly agree, but I fear it was not on a woman's account that I travelled down to Tresco. Dick I think had something to do with it, but chiefly I came to do myself a service."

"Well," she answered as she rose and crossed to the window "that may be. You are here at all events, in the house that is watched" and then she suddenly called me to her side. "Look," said she, "but keep well behind the curtain."

I looked across the water to a brown pile of rocks which was named Norwithel, and beyond Norwithel over St. Helen's Pool to the island of St. Helen's.

"Do you see?" she asked.

I saw the bare rock, the purple heather of St. Helen's, to the right a wide shining beach of Tean, and to the left stretching out into the sea from the end of St. Helen's a low ridge of rocks like a paved causeway. I pointed to that causeway.

"That is the Golden Ball Reef," said I.

"Yes," she answered, "Dick told you the story. You would not see the reef, but that the tide is low. But it is not that I wanted to show you. See!" and she stretched out her hand towards the rock pile of Norwithel.

I looked there again and at last I saw a man moving on the rocks close by the sea.

"He is cutting the weed," said I.

"That is the pretence," said she. "But so long as he stays there no one can enter this house without he knows, no one can go out without he knows."

"Unless one goes in or out by the door I used."

"That door is within view of the Castle Down,

There will be some man smoking his pipe, stretched on the grass of the Castle Down."

"You have never spoken to them?"

"Yes! They wanted nothing of me. They only watch. I know for whom they watch. I could learn nothing by questioning them."

"Have you asked Captain Hathaway's help?"

Helen smiled.

"No. What could he do? They do no one any hurt. They stand out of my way when I pass. And besides—I am afraid. I do not know. If these men were questioned closely by some one in authority, what story might they have to tell and what part in that story does Cullen play?"

I hesitated for a few moments whether to risk the words which were on my lips. I made an effort and spoke them.

"You will pardon the question—I have once met Cullen Mayle—and is he worth all this anxiety?"

"He had a strange upbringing in this house. There is much to excuse him in the eyes of any one. And for myself I cannot forget that all which people say is mine, is more rightly his."

She spoke very gently about Cullen, as I had indeed expected that she would, but with sufficient firmness to prove to me that it was not worth while to continue upon this strain.

"And the negro?" I asked. "He has not spoken?"

For answer she led me up the stairs, and into a room which opened upon the landing. The negro lay in bed and asleep. The flesh had shrivelled off his bones, his face was thin and peaked, and plainly his days were numbered. Helen leaned over the bed, spoke to him and pressed upon his shoulder. The negro opened his eyes. Never in my life had I seen anything so melancholy as their expression. The conviction of his helplessness was written upon them and I think too an appeal for forgiveness that he had not discharged his mission.

"Speak to him," said Helen. "Perhaps a stranger's voice may rouse him if only to speak two words."

I spoke to him as she bade me; a look of intelligence came into the negro's face; I put a question to him.

"Why does George Glen watch for Cullen Mayle?"—and before I had completed the sentence his eyelids closed languidly over his eyes and he was asleep. I looked at him as he lay there, an emaciated motionless figure, the white bedclothes against his ebony skin, and as I thought of his long travels ending so purposelessly in this captivity of sleep, I was filled with a great pity. Helen uttered a moan, she turned towards me wringing her hands.

"And there's our secret," she cried, "the secret which we must know and which this poor negro burns to tell and it's locked up within him! Bolts and bars," she burst out, "what puny things they seem! One can break bolts, one can sever bars, but a secret buried within a man, how shall one unearth it?"

It just occurred to me that she stopped with unusual abruptness, but I was looking at the negro, I was still occupied with pity.

"Heaven send my journey does not end so vainly as his," I said solemnly. I turned to Helen and I saw that she was staring at me with a great astonishment, and concern for which I could not account.

"I have a conjecture to tell you of," said I, "I do not know that it is of value."

"Let us go downstairs," she replied, "and you shall tell me," but she spoke slowly as though she was puzzled with some other matter. As we went downstairs I heard Dick Parmiter's voice and could understand the words he said. I stopped.

"Where is Dick?"

"Most likely in the kitchen."

When we were come to the foot of the stairs I asked where the kitchen was?

"At the end of that passage across the hall," she answered.

Upon that I called Dick. I heard a door open and shut, and Dick came into the hall.

"The kitchen door was closed," said I, "I do not know but what my conjecture may have some value after all."

Helen Mayle walked into the parlour, Dick followed her. As I crossed the hall my coat caught on the back of a chair. Whilst I was disengaging my coat, I noticed that an end of the white scarf was hanging from my pocket and that the initials "H. M." were embroidered upon it. I recollected then how Helen Mayle had abruptly ended her outcry concerning the bolts and bars, and how she had looked at me and how she had spoken. Had she noticed the scarf? I thrust it back into my pocket and took care that the flap of the pocket should hide it completely. Then I, too, went into the parlour. But as I entered the room I saw then Helen's eyes went at once to my pocket. She had, then, noticed the scarf. It seemed, however, that she was no longer perplexed as to how I came by it. But, on the other hand, it was my turn to be perplexed. For, as she raised her eyes from my pocket, our glances crossed. It was evident to her that I had detected her look and understood it. Yet she smiled—without any embarrassment; it was as though she thought I had stolen her scarf for a favour and she forgave the theft. And then she blushed. That, however, she was very ready to do upon all occasions.

CHAPTER IX

TELLS OF A STAIN UPON A WHITE FROCK, AND A LOST KEY

Helen drew a chair to the table and waited with her hands folded before her.

"Dick," said I, turning to the lad, who stood just within the door, "that oath of yours."

"I have broken it already," said he.

"There was never priest in the world who would refuse to absolve you. The virtue of it lies in the forswearing. Now!" and I turned to Helen. "But I must speak frankly," I premised.

She nodded her assent.

"Very well. I can make a consecutive sort of story, but I may well be at fault, for my knowledge is scanty, and if I am in error over the facts, I beg you, Miss Mayle, to correct me. Old Mr. Mayle's talk ran continually about his wild doings on the Guinea coast, in Africa. There can be no doubt that he spent some considerable portion of his life there, and that he managed to scrape together a sufficient fortune. It is likely, therefore, that he was engaged in the slave trade, and, to be quite frank, Miss Helen, from what I have gathered of his manner and style, I am not indisposed to think that he found an occasional diversion from that pursuit in a little opportune piracy."

I made the suggestion with some diffidence, for the old man, whatever his sins, had saved her life, and shown her much affection, of which, moreover, at his death he had given her very tangible proofs. It was necessary for me, however, to say it, for I had nothing but suspicion to go upon, and I looked to her in some way, either by words or manner, to confirm or confute my suspicions. And it seemed to me that she confirmed it, for she simply pressed the palms of her hands to her forehead, and said quietly,

"You are very frank."

"There is no other way but frankness, believe me," I returned. "Now let us come to that Sunday, four years ago, when Cullen Mayle sat in the stocks and George Glen came to Tresco. It was you who took George Glen to St. Mary's Church," I turned to Dick Parmiter.

"Yes," said he. "I was kicking my heels in

the sand, close to our cottage, when he came ashore in a boat. He was most anxious to speak with Mr. Mayle."

"So you carried him across to St. Mary's, and he told you, I think, that he had been quartermaster with Adam Mayle at Whydah, on the Guinea coast?"

"Yes."

"Did he name the ship by any chance?"

"No."

"He did once, whilst we were at supper," interrupted Helen, "and I remember the name very well, for my father turned upon him fiercely when he spoke it, and Mr. Glen immediately said that he was mistaken and substituted another name, which I have forgotten. The first name was the *Royal Fortune*."

"The *Royal Fortune*," said I, thoughtfully. The name in a measure was familiar to me; it seemed familiar too in precisely this connection with the Guinea coast. But I could not be sure. I was anxious to discover George Glen's business with Adam Mayle, and very likely my anxiety misled me into imagining clues where there were none. I put the name away in my mind and went on with my conjecture.

"Now on that Sunday George Glen met Adam Mayle in the churchyard, you, Miss Mayle, and Lieutenant Clutterbuck were of the party. Together you sailed across to Tresco. So that George Glen could have had no private word with Mr. Mayle."

"No," Helen Mayle agreed. "There was no opportunity."

"Nor was there an opportunity all that afternoon and evening, until Cullen left the house."

"But after Cullen had gone," said she, "they had their opportunity and made use of it. I left them together in my father's room.

"The room fitted up as a cabin, where every word they spoke could be heard though the door was shut and the eavesdropper need not even trouble to lay his ear to the keyhole."

"Yes, that is true," said Helen. "But the servants were in bed, and there was no one to hear."

At that Dick gave a start and a jump, and I cried:

"But there was some one to hear. Tell your story, Dick!" and Dick told how Cullen Mayle had climbed through the window, and how some hours after he had waked him up and sworn him to secrecy.

"Now, do you see?" I continued. "Why should Cullen Mayle have sworn Dick here to silence unless he had discovered some sort of secret which might prove of value to himself, unless he had overhead George Glen talking to Adam Mayle? And there's this besides. Where has Cullen Mayle been these last two years? I can tell you that."

"You can?" said Helen. She was leaning across the table, her face all lighted up with excitement.

"Yes. There's the negro above stairs for one thing, Cullen's servant. For another I met Cullen Mayle on the road as I was travelling here. He counterfeited an ague, which he told me he had caught on the Guinea coast. The ague was counterfeit, but very likely he has been on the Guinea coast."

"Of course," cried Dick.

"Not a doubt of it," said Helen.

"So this is my theory. George Glen came to enlist Adam Mayle's help and Adam Mayle's money, in some voyage to Africa. Cullen Mayle overheard it, and got the start of George Glen. So here's George Glen back again upon Tresco, and watching for Cullen Mayle."

"See!" cried Helen suddenly. "Did I not tell you you were sent here to a good end?"

"But we are not out of the wood yet," I protested. "We have to discover what it was that Glen proposed to Mr. Mayle. How shall we do that?"

"How?" repeated Helen, and she looked to me confidently for the answer.

"I can think of but one way," said I, "to go boldly to George Glen and make terms with him."

"Would he speak, do you think?"

"Most likely not," I answered, and so in spite of my fine conjecture, we did not seem to have come any nearer to an issue. We were both of us silent for some while. The very confidence which Helen displayed stung me into an activity of thought. Helen herself was sunk in an abstraction, and in that abstraction she spoke.

"You are hurt," she said.

My right hand was resting upon the table. It was cut in one or two places, and covered with scratches.

"It is nothing," said I, "I slipped on the hill yesterday night and cut it with the gorse;" and again we fell to silence.

"What I am thinking is this," she said, at

length. "You overtook Cullen upon the road, and you reached the islands last night. At any moment then we may expect his coming."

"Why, that's true," said I, springing up to my feet. "And if Dick will sail me across to St. Mary's, we'll make a shift to stop him."

Helen Mayle rose at that moment from her seat. She was wearing a white frock, and upon one side of it I noticed for the first time a red smear or two, as though she had brushed against paint—or blood. I looked at my hand scratched and torn by the gorse bush. It would have been bleeding at the time when a woman, coming swiftly past us in the fog, brushed against it. The woman was certainly hurrying in the direction of this house.

"You have told me everything, I suppose," I said—"everything at all events that it concerns me to know."

"Everything," she replied.

We crossed that afternoon to St. Mary's. There was no sign of Cullen Mayle at Hugh Town. No one had seen him or heard of his coming. He had not landed upon St. Mary's. I thought it possible that he might not have touched St. Mary's at all, but rowed ashore to Tresco even as I had done. But no ship had put into the Road that day but one which brought Castile soap from Marseilles. We sailed back to Tresco, and ran the boat's nose into the sand not twenty yards from the door of the house on Merchant's Point. A man, an oldish, white-haired man, loitering upon the beach very civilly helped us to run the boat up out of the water. We thanked him, and he touched his hat and answered with something of a French accent, which surprised me. But as we walked up to the house,

"That's one of the five," Dick explained. "He came on the boat with the negro to Penzance. Peter Tortue he is called, and he was loitering there on purpose to get a straight look at you."

"Well," said I, "it is at all events known that I am here," and going into the house I found Helen Mayle eagerly waiting for our return. I told her that Cullen Mayle could not by any means have yet reached the Scillies, and that we had left word with the harbour master upon St. Mary's to detain him if he landed; at which she expressed great relief.

"And since it is known I am here," I added, "it will be more suitable if I carry my valise over to New Grimsby and seek a bed at the 'Palace'

Inn. I shall besides make the acquaintance of Mr. George Glen. It is evident that he and his fellows intend no hurt to you, so that you may sleep in peace."

"No," said she, bravely enough. "I am not afraid for myself."

"And you will do that?"

"What?" she asked.

"Sleep in peace," said I; and putting my hand into my pocket as if by accident, I let her see again the corner of her white scarf. Her face flushed a little as she saw it.

"Oh, yes," she answered, and to my surprise with the easiest laugh imaginable. "I shall sleep in peace. You need have no fear."

I could not understand her. What a passion of despair it must have needed to string her to that act of death last night! Yet to-day—she could even allude to it with a laugh. I was lost in perplexity, but I had this one sure thing to comfort me. She was to-day hopeful, however much she despaired yesterday. She relied upon me to rescue Cullen from his peril. I was not sure that I should be doing her the service she imagined it to be, even if I succeeded. But she loved him, and looked to me to help her. So that I, too, could sleep in peace without fear that to-night another scarf would be fetched out to do the office this one I kept had failed to do.

 I gave Dick my valise to carry across the island, and waited until he was out of sight before I started. Then I walked to the palisade at the end of the house. I found a spot where the palisade was broken; the splintered wood was fresh and clean; it was I who had broken the palisade last night. From that point I marched straight up the hill through the gorse, and when I had walked for about twenty minutes I stopped and looked about me. I struck away to my left, and after a little I stopped again. I marched up and down that hill, to the right, to the left, for perhaps the space of an hour, and at last I came upon that for which I searched—a steep slope where the grass was crushed, and underneath that slope a sheer descent. On the brink of the precipice—for that I judged it to be—I saw a broken gorse-bush. I lay down on my face and carefully crawled down the slope. The roots of the gorse-bush still held firmly in the ground. I clutched it in my left hand, dug the nails of my right through the grass into the soil and leaned over. My precipice was no more than a hollow some twenty feet deep, and had I slipped yesterday night, I should not have fallen even those twenty feet; for a sort of low barn was built in the hollow, with its back leaning against the perpendicular wall. I should have dropped perhaps ten feet on to the roof of this barn.

I drew myself up the hill again and sat down. The evening was very quiet and still. I was near to the summit of the island. Over my left shoulder I could see the sun setting far away in the Atlantic, and the waves rippling gold. Beneath me was the house, a long one-storied building of granite, on the horn of a tiny bay. The windows looked across the bay; behind the house stretched that tangled garden, and at the end of the garden rose the Merchant's Rock. As it stood thus in the evening light, with the smoke curling from its chimneys, and the sea murmuring at its door, it seemed quite impossible to believe that any story of turmoil and strife and tragedy could have locality there. That old buccaneer Adam Mayle, and his soft-voiced son Cullen, whom he had turned adrift, seemed the figures of a dream and my adventure in Cullen's room—a hideous nightmare.

And yet even as I looked footsteps brushed

through the grass behind me, and turning I saw a sailor with a brass telescope under one arm and a black patch over one eye; who politely passed me the time of day and went by. He was a big man, with a great beard and hair sprouting from his ears and nostrils. He was another of the five no doubt, and though he went by he did not pass out of sight. I waited, hoping that he would go, for I had a great desire to examine the barn beneath me more closely. It was from the barn that the unearthly screeching had risen which had so terrified Dick Parmiter. It was between the barn and the house that a girl had brushed against my wounded hand and taken a stain of blood upon her dress.

The hollow was only a break in the steep slope of the hill. The barn could easily be approached by descending the hill to the right or the left, and then turning in. I was anxious to do it, to try the door, to enter the barn, but I dared not, for the sailor was within sight, and I had no wish to arouse any suspicions. Helen had told me everything, she had said—everything which it concerned me to know. But had she? I found myself asking, as I got to my feet and crossed the hill down towards New Grimsby.

The sun had set by this time, a cool twilight took the colour from the gorse, and numberless small winged things flew and sung about one's face; all round a grey sea went down to a grey sky, and sea and sky were merged; and at my feet the lights began to twinkle in the little fishing village by the sea. I hired a bed at the "Palace" Inn, bade them prepare me supper and then walked on to Parmiter's cottage for my valise.

There was a great hubbub going on within; Dick's voice was explaining, and a woman's shrill voice overtopped his explanation. The cause of his offence was twofold. He had not been near the cottage all day, so that it was thought he had run away again, and the key of the cottage was gone. It had not been seen since yesterday, and Dick had been accused of purloining it. I explained to Mrs. Parmiter that it was my fault Dick had kept away all day, and I made a bargain with her that I should have the lad as my servant while I stayed upon the island. Dick shouldered my valise in a state of considerable indignation.

"What should I steal the key for?" said he. "It only stands in the door for show. No one locks his door in Tresco. What should I steal the key for?" and he was within an ace of whimpering.

"Come, Dick," said I, "you mustn't mind a trifle of a scolding. Why, you are a hero to everybody in these parts, and to one man at all events outside them."

"That doesn't hinder mother from chasing me about with an oar," he answered."

"It is the fate of all heroes," said I, "to be barbarously used by their womenfolk."

"Then I am damned if I want to be a hero," said Dick, violently. "And as for the key—of what consequence is it at all if you never lock your door?"

"Of no more consequence than your bruises, Dick," said I.

But I was wrong. You may do many things with a key besides locking a door. You can slip it down your back to stop your nose bleeding, for instance; if it's a big key you can weigh a line with it, and perhaps catch a mackerel for your breakfast. And there's another use for a key of which I did not at this time know, or I should have been saved from considerable perplexity and not a little danger.

CHAPTER X

IN WHICH I LEARN SOMETHING FROM AN ILL-PAINTED PICTURE

I TOOK my supper in the kitchen of the Palace Inn, with a strong reek of tobacco to season it, and a succession of gruesome stories to make it palatable. The company was made up for the most part of fishermen, who talked always of wrecks upon the western islands and of dead men drowned. But occasionally a different accent and a different anecdote of some other corner of the world would make a variation; and doing my best to pierce the haze of smoke, I recognised the speaker as Peter Tortue, the Frenchman, or the man with the patch on his eye. George Glen was there too, tucked away in a corner by the fireplace, but he said very little. I paid, therefore, but a scanty attention, until, the talk having slid, as it will, from dead men to their funerals, some native began to descant upon the magnificence of Adam Mayle's.

"Ay," said he, drawing a long breath, "there *was* a funeral, and all according to orders dictated in writing by the dead man. He was to be buried by torchlight in the Abbey Grounds. I do remember that! Mortal heavy he was, and he needed a big coffin."

"To be sure he would," chimed in another.

"And he had it too," said a third; "a mortal big coffin. We carried him right from his house over the shoulder of the island, and down past the Abbey pond to the graveyard. Five shillings each we had for carrying him—five shillings counted out by torchlight on a gravestone as soon as the grave was filled in. It was all written down before he died."

Then the first speaker took up the tale again.

"A queer, strange man was Adam Mayle, and queer strange sights he had seen. He would sit in that corner just where you be, Mr. Glen, and tell stories to turn a man cold. Crackers they used to call him on board ship, so he told us—'Crackers.'"

"Why Crackers?" asked George Glen.

"'Cause he was that handy with a marlinspike. A queer man! And that was a queer notion of his about that stick"; and then he appealed to his companions, who variously grunted their assent.

"What about the stick?" asked Glen.

"You may well ask, Mr. Glen. It was all written down. The stick was to be buried with him in his coffin. It was an old heavy stick with a great brass handle. Many's the time he has sat on the settle there with that stick atween his knees. 'Twas a stick with a sword in't, but the sword was broken. I remember how he loosened the handle once while he was talking just as you and I are now, and he held the stick upside down and the sword fell out on to the ground, just two or three inches of steel broken off short. He picked it up pretty sharp and rammed it in again. Well, the stick was to be buried with him, so that if he woke up when we were carrying him over the hill to the Abbey he might knock on the lid of his coffin."

"But I doubt if any one would ha' opened the lid if he had knocked," said one, with a chuckle, and another nodded his head to the sentiment. "There was five shillings, you see," he explained, "once the ground was stamped down on top of him. It wasn't quite human to expect a body to open the lid."

"A queer notion—about that stick."

And so the talk drifted away to other matters. The fishermen took their leave one by one and tramped heavily to their homes. Peter Tortue and his companion followed. George Glen alone remained, and he sat so quiet in his corner that I forgot his presence. Adam Mayle was the only occupant of the room for me. I could see him sitting on the settle, with a long pipe between his lips when he was not holding a mug there, his mulberry face dimly glowing through the puffs of tobacco, and his voice roaring out those wild stories of the African coast. That anxiety for a barbaric funeral seemed quite a piece with the man as my fancies sketched him. Well, he was lying in the Abbey grounds, and George Glen sat in his place.

Mr. Glen came over to me from his corner, and I called for a jug of rum punch, and invited him to share it, which he willingly did. He was a little squabby man, but very broad, with a nervous twitting laugh, and in his manner he was extremely intimate and confidential. He could hardly finish a sentence without plucking you by the sleeve, and every commonplace he uttered was pointed with a wink. He knew that I had been

AN ILL-PAINTED PICTURE 143

over at the house under Merchant's Rock, and he was clumsily inquisitive about my business upon Tresco.

"Why," said I, indifferently, "I take it that I am pretty much in the same case with you, Mr. Glen."

At that his jaw dropped a little, and he stared at me utterly discountenanced that I should be so plain with him.

"As for me," said he in a little, "it is plain enough. And when you say"—and here he twitched my sleeve as he leaned across the table—"'here's old George Glen, that battered about the world in ships for fifty years, and has come to his moorings in a snug harbor where rum's cheap, being smuggled or stole', says you—well, I am not denying you may be right;" and here he winked prodigiously.

"And that's just what I said," I returned; "for here have I battered about London, that's worse than the sea, and ages a man twice as fast——"

Mr. Glen interrupted me with some astonishment, and, I thought, a little alarm.

"Why," says she, "this is no place for the likes of you—a crazy tumbledown of a tavern. All very well for tarry sailor folk that's never seen nothing better than forecastle. But you'll sicken of it in a week. Sure, you have not dropped your anchor here."

"We'll call it a kedge, Mr. Glen," said I.

"A kedge, you say," answered Mr. Glen, with a titter, "and a kedge we'll make it. It's a handy thing to get on board in a hurry."

He spoke with a wheedling politeness, but very likely a threat underlay his words. I thought it wise to take no notice of them, but, rising from my seat, I wished him good night. And there the conversation would have ended but for a couple of pictures upon the wall which caught my eye.

One was the ordinary picture which you may come upon in a hundred alehouses by the sea: the sailor leaving his cottage for a voyage, his wife and children clinging about his knees, and in the distance an impossible ship unfurling her sails upon an impossible ocean. The second, however, it was, which caught my attention. It was the picture of a sailor's return. His wife and children danced before him, he was clad in magnificent garments, and to prove the prosperity of his voyage he carried in his hand a number of gold watches and chains; and the artist, whether it was that he had a sense of humour or that he merely doubted his talents, instead of painting the watches, had cut holes in the canvas and inserted little discs of bright metal.

"This is a new way of painting pictures, Mr. Glen," said I.

Mr. Glen's taste in pictures was crude, and for these he expressed a quite sentimental admiration.

"But," I objected, "the artist is guilty of a libel, for he makes the sailor out to be a sneak-thief."

Mr. Glen became indignant.

"Because he comes home with wealth untold?" he asked grandly.

"No, but because he comes home with watches," said I.

Whereupon Mr. Glen was at some pains to explain to me that the watches were merely symbolical.

"And the picture's true," he added, and fell to pinching my arm. "There's many a landsman laughs; but sailors, you says, says you, 'comes home with watches in their 'ands more than they can 'old and sets up for gentle-folk,' says you."

"Like old Adam Mayle, I adds," said I; and

Mr. Glen dropped my arm and stood a little way off blinking at me.

"You knew Adam?" he said, in a fierce sort of way.

"No," I answered.

"But you know of him?"

"Yes," said I, slowly, "I know of him, but not as much as you do, Mr. Glen, who were quartermaster with him at Whydah on the ship *Royal Fortune*."

I spoke at random, wondering how he would take the words, and they had more effect than I had even hoped for. His face turned all of a mottled colour; he banged his fist upon the table and uttered a horrible oath, calling upon God to slay him if he had ever set foot on the deck of a ship named the *Royal Fortune*.

"And when you says, says you," he added, sidling up to me, "Old George never see'd a *Royal Fortune*, says you—why, you're saying what's right and fair, and I thanks you, sir. I thanks you with a true sailor's 'eart"; at which he would have wrung my hand. But I had no hand ready for him; I barely heard his words. Whydah—the Guinea coast—the ship *Royal Fortune!* The truth came so suddenly upon me that

AN ILL-PAINTED PICTURE

I had not the wit to keep silence. I could have bitten off my tongue the next moment. As it was I caught most of the sentence back. But the beginning of it jumped from my mouth.

"At last I know"—I began and stopped.

"What?" said Mr. Glen, with his whole face distorted into an insinuating grin. But he was standing very close to me and a little behind my back.

"That my father thrashed me over twenty years ago," said I, clapping my hand to my coat tails and springing away from him.

"And you have never forgotten it," said he.

"On the contrary," said I, "I have only just remembered it."

Mr. Glen moved away from the table and walked towards the door. Thus he disclosed the table to me, and I laughed very contentedly. Mr. Glen immediately turned. He had reached the door, and he stood in the doorway biting shreds of skin from his thumb.

"You are in good spirits," said he, rather surlily.

"I was never in better," said I. "The motions of inanimate bodies are invariably instructive."

I was very willing he should think me half-witted. He went grumbling up the stairs; I turned me again to the picture of the sailor's return. Whydah—the Guinea coast—the ship *Royal Fortune!* It may have been in some part the man's eagerness to deny all knowledge of the ship; it was, no doubt, in some part the picture of those gold watches, which awakened my memories. Watches of just such gold were dangling for sale on a pedler's stall when first I heard of the ship *Royal Fortune.* The whole scene came back to me most vividly—the market-place of an old country town upon a fair day, the carts, the crowds, the merry-go-rounds, the pedler's stall with the sham gold watches, and close by the stall a ragged hawker singing a ballad of the *Royal Fortune*, and selling copies of the ballad—a ballad to which was added the last confessions of four men hung for piracy at Cape Coast Castle within the flood-marks. It was well over twenty years since that day, but I remembered it now with a startling distinctness. There was a rough woodcut upon the title-page of the ballad representing four men hanging in chains upon four gibbets. I had bought one that afternoon, and my father had taken it from me and thrashed me soundly for reading it. But I had read it! My memory was quickened now to an almost supernatural clearness. I could almost turn over the pages in my mind and read it again. All four men—one of them was named Ashplant, a second Moody—went to the gallows without any sign of penitence. There was a third so grossly stupid—yes, his name was Hardy—so stupid that during his last moments he could think of nothing more important than the executioner's tying his wrists behind his back, and his last words were before they swung him off to the effect that he had seen many men hanged, but none with their hands tied in this way. The fourth—I could not recall his name, but he swore very heartily, saying that he would rather go to hell than to heaven, since he would find no pirates in heaven to keep him company, and that he would give Roberts a salute of thirteen guns at entrance. There was the story of a sea-fight, too, besides the ballad and the confessions and it all cost no more than a penny. What a well-spent penny! The fourth man's name, by-the-bye, was Sutton.

But the sea-fight! It was fought not many miles from Whydah between His Majesty's ship *Swallow* and the *Royal Fortune;* for the *Royal Fortune* was sailed by Captain Bartholomew Roberts, the famous pirate who was killed in this very encounter. How did George Glen or Adam Mayle or Peter Tortue (for he alone of Glen's assistants was of an age to have shipped on the *Royal Fortune*) escape? I did not care a button. I had my thumb on George Glen, and was very well content.

There was no doubt I had my thumb on the insinuating George. There was Adam Mayle's fortune, in the first place; there was Adam's look when George Glen let slip the name of the ship when he first came to Tresco; there was Glen's consternation this evening when I repeated it to him, and there was something more than his convincing than his consternation—a table-knife.

He had come very close to me when I mentioned the *Royal Fortune*, and he had stood a little behind me—against the table at which I had eaten my supper. I had eaten that supper at the opposite side of the table, and how should a table-knife have crawled across the table and be now lying so handily on this nearer edge unless George had doubts of my discretion? Yes, I had my thumb upon him and as I went upstairs to bed I wondered whether after all Helen would be justified of her confidence in believing that I had been sent to Tresco to some good end. Her face was very present to me that night. There was much in her which I could not understand. There was something, too, to trouble one, there were concealments, it almost seemed there was a trace of effrontery—such as Lieutenant Clutterbuck had spoken of; but to-night I was conscious chiefly that she set her faith in me and my endeavours. Does the reed always break if you lean upon it? What if a miracle happened and the reed grew strong because some one—any one—leaned upon it! I kept that trustful face of hers as I had seen it in the sunlight, long before my eyes in the darkness of the room. But it changed, as I knew and feared it would,—it changed to that appalling face which had stared at me out of the dark. I tried to drive that picture of her from my thoughts.

But I could not, until a door creaked gently. I sat up in my bed with a thought of that knife handy on the table edge to the grasp of George Glen. I heard a scuffle of shoeless feet draw towards my door, and I remembered that I had no weapon—not even a knife. The feet stopped at my door, and I seemed to hear the sound of breathing. The moon had already sunk, but the night was clear, and I watched the white door and the white woodwork of the door frame. The door was in the wall on my right; it was about midway between the head and the foot of my bed, and it opened inwards and down towards the foot; so that I should easily see it opening. But suddenly I heard the stair boards creaking. Whoever it was then, had merely stopped to listen at my door. I fell back on my bed with a relief so great as to surprise me. I was surprised, too, to find myself cold with sweat. I determined to buy myself a knife in the morning, for there was the girl over at Merchant's Point who looked to me. I had thus again a picture of her in the sunlight.

And then I began to wonder at that stealthy descent of the stairs. And why should any one wish to assure himself I slept? This was a question to be looked into. I got out of bed very cautiously, as cautiously opened the door and peered out.

There was a light burning in the kitchen—a small yellow light as of a candle, but I could hear no sound. I crept to the head of the stairs which were steep and led directly to the very threshold of the kitchen. I lay down on the boards of the landing and stretching my head down the stairs, looked into the room.

George Glen had taken the sailor with the watches, down from the wall. He was seated with the candle at his elbow, and minutely examining the picture. He looked up towards the stairs, I drew my face quickly back; but he was gazing in a complete abstraction, and biting his thumb, very much puzzled. I crept back to bed and in a little I heard him come shuffling up the stairs. He had been examining that picture to find a reason for my exclamation. It was a dull-witted thing to do and I could have laughed at him heartily, only I had already made a mistake in taking him to be duller-witted than he was. For he was quick enough, at all events, to entertain suspicions.

CHAPTER XI

OUR PLANS MISCARRY UPON CASTLE DOWN

THE next morning, you may be sure, I crossed the hill betimes, and came down to the house under Merchant's Rock with my good news. I told her the news with no small elation, and with a like elation she began to hear it. But as I related what had occurred at the Palace Inn, she fell into thought, and now smiled with a sort of pride, and now checked a sigh; and when I came to the knife upon the table's edge she shuddered.

"But you are in danger!" she cried. "Every minute you are in danger of your life, and on my account!"

"Nay," said I lightly, "you exaggerate. The best of women have that fault."

But she did not smile. She laid a hand upon my arm, and said, very earnestly:

"I cannot have it. I am very proud you count the risk so little, but you must go."

"No," said I, "they must go, and we have the means to make them march. We have but to inform Captain Hathaway at the Garrison that here are some of Bartholomew Robert's fry, and we and the world will soon be quit of them for ever."

"But we cannot," she exclaimed, "for then it would be known that my"—she hesitated for a second, or rather she paused, for there was no hesitation in her voice, as she continued—"my father also was of the band. It may be justice that it should be known. But I cannot help it; I guard his memory. Besides, there is Cullen."

It was to Cullen that she always came in the end, and with such excuses as a girl might make who was loyal to a man whom she must know not to be worth her loyalty. The house in which she lived, the money which she owned were his by right. She dreaded what story these men, if captured, might have to tell of Cullen—she could not be persuaded that Glen and his friends had not a motive of vengeance as well as of gain,— and that story, whatever it was, would never have been enacted, had not Cullen been driven penniless from Tresco. It did not occur to her at all that this house was not Cullen's by any right, but belonged to the scattered sons of many men with whom the ship *Royal Fortune* had fallen in.

She repeated her arguments to me as we walked in the grass-grown garden at the back of the house. A thick shrubbery of trees grew at the end of the garden, and behind the trees rose the Merchant's Rock. On one side the Castle Down rolled up towards the sky, on the other a hedge closed the garden in, and beneath the hedge was the sea. Over the hedge I could see the uninhabited island of St. Helen's and the ruined church upon the summit, and a ship or two in St. Helen's Pool; and this side of the ships the piled boulders of Norwithel. It was at Norwithel that I looked as she spoke, and when she had done I continued:

"I do not propose that we should tell Captain Hathaway, but I can make a bargain with Glen. I can find out what he wants, and strike a bargain with him. We have the upper hand, we can afford to speak freely. I will make a bargain with him to-night, of which one condition shall be that he and his party leave Tresco and nowhere attempt to molest Cullen Mayle."

But she stopped in front of me.

"I cannot have it," she said, with energy.

"This means danger to you who propose the bargain."

"I shall propose it in the inn kitchen," said I.

"And the knife on the table's edge?" she asked; "that too was in the inn kitchen. Oh, no! no!" she cried, in a voice of great trouble. There was great trouble too in her eyes.

"Madam," I said, gently, "I never thought that this would prove a schoolboy's game. If I had thought so, I should be this instant walking down St. James's. But you overrate my peril."

I saw her draw herself erect.

"No; it is I who will propose the bargain and make the conditions. It is I who will charge them with their piracy."

"How?" I asked.

"I will go this morning to the Palace Inn."

"George Glen went out this morning before I rose."

She looked over to Norwithel.

"There is no one to-day on Norwithel," said I.

"I shall find Peter Tortue on the Castle Down."

"But I crossed the Castle Down this morning ——" and I suddenly stopped. There had been no one watching on the Castle Down. There was no one anywhere upon the watch to-day. The significance of this omission struck me then for the first time.

"What if already we are quit of them!" I cried. "What if that one tiny word *Royal Fortune* has sent them at a scamper into hiding?"

Helen caught something of my excitement.

"Oh! if it only could be so!" she exclaimed.

"Most like it *is* so," I returned. "No man cutting ore-weed upon Norwithel! No man lounging on the Castle Down! It must be so!" and we shook hands upon that likelihood as though it was a certainty. We started guiltily apart the next moment, for a servant came into the garden with word that Dick Parmiter had sailed round in a boat from New Grimsby, and was waiting for me.

"There is something new!" said Helen, clasping her hands over her heart, and in a second she was all anxiety. I hastened to reassure her. Dick had come at my bidding, for I was minded to sail over to St. Mary's, and discover if there was anywhere upon that island a record of the doings of the *Royal Fortune*. To that end I asked Helen to give me a letter to the chaplain there, who would be likely to know more of what happened up and down the world than the natives of the islands. I was not, however, to allow that I had any particular interest in the matter, lest the Rev. Mr. Milray should smell a rat as they say, and on promising to be very exact in this particular and to return to the house in time for supper, I was graciously given the letter.

I found the Rev. Mr. Milray in his parsonage at Old Town, a small, elderly man, who would talk of nothing but the dampness of his house since the great wave which swept over this neck of land on the day of the earthquake at Lisbon. I left him very soon, therefore, and went about another piece of business.

I had travelled from London with no more clothes and linen than a small valise would hold. On setting out, I had not considered, indeed, that I should be thrown much into the company of a lady, but only that I was journeying into a rough company of fisher-folk. Yesterday, however, it had occurred to me that I must make some addition to my wardrobe and the necessity was yet more apparent to-day. I was pleased, therefore, to find that Hugh Town was of greater importance than I had thought it to be. It is much shrunk and dwindled now, but then ships from all quarters of the world were continually putting in there, so that they made a trade by themselves, and there was always for sale a great store of things which had been salved from wrecks. I was able, therefore, to fit myself out very properly.

I sailed back to the Palace Inn, dressed with some care, and walked over to sup at Merchant's Rock—little later perhaps. Helen Mayle was standing in the hall by the foot of the stairs. I saw her face against the dark panels as I entered, and it looked very white and strained with fear.

"There is no news of Cullen at St. Mary's," I said, to lighten her fears; and she showed an extravagant relief, before, indeed, she could barely have heard the words. Her face coloured brightly and then she began to laugh. Finally she dropped me a curtsey.

"Shall I lend you some hair-powder?" she asked, whimsically; and when we were seated at table, "How old are you?"

"I was thirty and more a month ago," said I, "but I think that I am now only twenty-two."

"As much as that?" said she, with a laugh, and grew serious in an instant. "What did you discover at St. Mary's besides a milliner?"

"Nothing," said I, "except that the Rev. Milray suffers from the rheumatics."

She remained in the same variable disposition during the whole of that supper, at one moment buoyant on a crest of light-heartedness and her eyes sparkling like stars, at another sunk into despondency and her white brows all wrinkled with frowns. But when supper was over she went to a cabinet, and taking from it a violin, said:

" Now, I will play to you."

And she did—out in that tangled garden over the sea.

" The violin came to the Scillies in a ship that was wrecked upon the Stevel Rock one Christmas. But the violin will tell you," she said, with a smile. " My father bought it at St. Mary's and gave it to me, and an old pilot now dead taught me;" and she swept the bow across the strings and the music trembled across the water, through the lucent night, up to the stars, a voice vibrating with infinite wisdom and infinite passion.

It seemed to me that I had at last got the truth of her. All my guesses, my suspicions of something like duplicity, even my recollection of our first meeting were swept out of my mind. She sat, her white face gleaming strangely solemn under her black wealth of hair, her white hand flashing backwards and forwards, and she made the violin speak. It spoke of all things, things most sad and things most joyous; it spoke with complete knowledge of the heights and the depths; it woke new, vague, uncomprehended hungers in one's heart; it called and called till all one's most sacred memories rose up, as it were from graves, to answer the summons. It told me, I know, all my life, from my childhood in the country to the day when I set out with my cadet's portion to London. It sang with almost a pæan of those first arduous years—set them to a march, —and then with a great pity told of those eight wasted years that followed—years littered with cards, stained with drink; years in which, and there was the humiliation of it, my fellow-drunkards, my fellow-gamblers had all been younger than myself—years in which I grew a million years old. That violin told it all out to me, until I twisted in my chair through sheer shame, and I looked up and the girl's eyes were fixed upon me. What it was that compelled me to speak I could never tell, unless it was the violin. But as she looked at me, and as that violin sobbed out its notes, I cried in a passionate excuse:

"You asked me how old I was. Do you know

I never was young—I never had the chance of youth! When the chance came, I had forgotten what youth can do. That accounts, surely, for those eight years. I was tired then, and I was never young."

"Until to-night," she said quietly, and the music quickened. I suppose that she was right, for I had never spoken so intimately to any one, whether man or woman; and I cursed myself for a fool, as one does when one is first betrayed into speaking of one's secret self.

She took the violin from her shoulder, and the glory of the music died off the sea, but lingered for a little faintly upon the hills. I rose up to go and Helen drew a breath and shivered.

"This afternoon," said I, "a brig went out from the islands through Crow Sound, bound for Milford. I'll wager the five were on it."

"But if not?"

"There's the 'Palace' kitchen."

"Speak when there are others by, not within hearing, but within reach! You will? Promise me!"

I promised readily enough, thinking that I could keep the promise, and she walked back with me through the house to the door. There is a little porch at the door, four wooden beams and a slate roof on the top, and half a dozen stone steps from the porch to the garden. Helen Mayle stood in the porch, with her violin still in her hand. She wished me "Good-night" when I was at the bottom of the steps, but a little afterwards, when I had passed through the gateway of the palisade and had begun to ascend the hill, she drew the bow sharply across one of the strings and sent a little chirp of music after me, which came to my ears, with an extraordinarily friendly sound. The air was still hereabouts, though from the motion of the clouds there was some wind in the sky, and the chirp came very clear and pretty.

It was a few minutes short of ten when I left the house, and I set off at a good pace, for I was anxious to keep my promise and make my bargain with George Glen, quietly in a corner, before the fishing-folk had gone home to bed. A young moon hung above the crest of the hill, a few white clouds were gathering towards it, and the gorse at my feet was black as ink. I walked upwards then steadily. I had walked for perhaps a quarter of an hour, when I heard a low, soft whistle. It came to me quite as clearly as the chirp of the violin, but it had not the same friendly sound. It sounded very lonesome, it set my heart jumping, it brought me to a stop. For I had heard precisely that whistle on one occasion before, on the night when I first crossed this hill with Dick Parmiter down to Merchant's Rock.

The whistle had sounded from below me and from no great distance away. I turned and looked down the slope, but I could see no one. It was very lonely and very still. Whoever had whistled lay crouched on the gorse. And then the whistle sounded again, but this time it came from above me, higher up the slope. Immediately I dropped to the ground. The gorse which hid them from me might well hide me from them. A few paces above me the gorse seemed thicker than it was where I lay. I crawled laboriously, flat upon my face, till I reached this patch. I forced myself into it, holding my face well down to keep the thorns out of my eyes, until the bushes were so close I could crawl no further. Then I lay still as a mouse, holding my breath, listening with every nerve. I had eluded them before in just this way, but I got little comfort from that reflection. There had been a fog on that night, whereas to-night it was clear. Moreover, they had a more urgent reason now for persevering in their search. I possessed some dangerous knowledge about them as they were aware—knowledge, too dangerous; knowledge which would harden into a weapon in my hand if—if I reached the Palace Inn alive.

I lay very still, and in a little I heard the brushing of their feet through the grass. They were closing down from above, they were closing up from below; but they did not speak or so much as whisper. I turned my head sideways, ever so gently, and looked up to the sky. I saw to my delight that the clouds were over the moon. I buried my face again in the grass, lest they should detect me by its pallor against the black gorse. I was very thankful indeed that I had not accepted that proffered loan of hair-powder—I was dressed in black, too, from head to foot; I blessed the good fortune which had led me to buy black stockings at St. Mary's, and, in a word, my hopes began to revive.

The feet came nearer, and I heard a voice whisper:

"It was here." The voice was Peter Tortue's, as I knew from the French accent, and the next instant a stick fell with a heavy thud not a foot from my head. If only the clouds hung in front of the moon! Round and about they tramped—the whole five of them. For in a little they began in low tones to curse, first of all me, and afterwards Peter Tortue, who had whistled from below. Let them only quarrel amongst themselves, I thought, and there's a good chance they will forget the reason of their quarrel. It seemed that they were well on the road to a quarrel at last; a man, quite young as I judged from his voice, flung himself down on the grass with an oath.

"But he is here, close to us," said Peter. "I heard the girl thrum good-night to him on her fiddle, and then I saw him, and followed him, and whistled."

"Well, it is your business, not mine. Yours and George Glen's," the other returned. I learned later that his name was Nathaniel Roper. "I was never on no *Royal Fortune*, devil damn me."

"Whist, you lousy fool"—and this was George Glen speaking. I am sure he was winking and pinching the fellow's arm,—"we are all in the same boat whether we've sailed in the *Royal*——" and he stopped.

All at once there was a dead silence. I have never in my life experienced anything so horrible as that sudden, complete silence. I could not see what caused it, for my face was buried in the grass, and I dared not move. One moment I had a sensation that they were gazing at my back, and I felt—it is the only way I can express it—I felt *naked*. Another moment I imagined it to be a ruse to beguile me into stirring; and it lasted for ever and ever.

At length one sound—not a voice—broke the silence: the man who had thrown himself down was getting to his feet. But when he had stood up he made no further movement; he stood motionless, like the others, and the silence began again and again it lasted for ever and ever.

All sorts of tremors began to creep over my body; the muscles of my back jerked of their own accord. The suspense was driving me mad. I had to move, I had to *see*, if only to hinder myself from leaping to my feet and making a headlong rush. Very slowly I turned my head sideways; I looked backwards along the ground, until I saw. The moon had swum out from the clouds, and the five men were standing in arrested attitudes with their eyes fixed upon something that glittered very bright upon the ground. I could see it myself through the gorse glittering and burning white, like a delicate flame, and my heart gave a great leap within me as I understood what it was. It was a big silver shoe-buckle that shone in the moonlight, and the shoe-buckle was on my foot.

The game was up. I thought that I might as well make a fight of it at the last, and I jumped to my feet suddenly, with a faint hope that the suddenness of the movement might startle them and let me through. But there was to be no fighting for me that night. It is true that the men all scattered from about me, but a voice a few yards to my right thundered, "Stand!" and I stood stock-still, obedient as a charity-school boy.

For Peter Tortue was standing stock still too, with his right arm stretched out in a line with his shoulder and the palm of his hand upturned. On the palm of that hand was balanced a long knife with an open blade, and the moonlight streaked along that blade in flame, just as it had burned upon my shoe-buckle.

George Glen rubbed his hands together.

"You will lie down, Mr. Berkeley," said he, with his most insinuating smile. "You will down, 'flat on my face,' says you."

"But I have only just got up," said I.

Glen tittered nervously, but no one else showed

any appreciation of my sally. I thought it best to lie down flat on my face.

"Cross your hands behind your back," said George Glen, and I knew he was winking.

"Any little thing like that, I am sure," I murmured, as I obeyed. "Only too happy," and in a trice I was nothing more than a coil of rope. It cut into my wrists, it crushed my chest, it snaked round my legs, it bit my ankles.

"To be sure," said I, "they mean to send me somewhere by the post."

Mr. George Glen sniggered and mentioned my destination, which was impolite, though he mentioned it politely; but Roper thumped me in the small of the back, and thrust my handkerchief into my mouth. So I had done better to have kept silence.

Two of the men lifted me up on their shoulders and staggered up hill. In a moment or two they descended a small incline, and I saw that I was being carried into the hollow where the shed stood. Glen pushed at the door of the shed and it fell open inwards. A great cavern of blackness gaped at us, and they carried me in and set me down unceremoniously on the floor.

"Brisk along with that lantern, Nat Roper,"

said Glen, and the young fellow who had flung himself down on the grass struck a light and set fire to the candle. The shed was divided by a wooden partition, in which was a rickety door hardly hanging on its hinges.

"In there!" said Glen, swinging the lantern towards the inner room. My bearers picked me up again and carried me to the door. One of them kicked at the door, but it did not yield.

"It's jammed," said the other, "there's something 'twixt it and the floor," and raising a great sea boot, he kicked with all his might.

I heard a metallic clinking, as though a piece of iron was hopping across the stone floor, and the door flew open.

They carried me into the inner room and set me down against the partition. There was no furniture of any sort, not even a bucket to sit upon; there was no window either, a thatched roof rested upon heavy beams over my head. They placed the lantern at my feet, four of them squatted down about me, the fifth went out of the shed to keep watch.

It was, after all, not in the inn kitchen of the Palace Inn that any bargain was to be struck. I could not deny that they had chosen their place very well. Not a man in Tresco but would give this shed the widest of berths, and if he saw the glint of this lantern through a chink, or heard, perhaps, as he was like to do, one loud cry—why, he would only take to his heels the faster. The ropes, too, made my bones ache.

I would have preferred the kitchen at the Palace Inn.

CHAPTER XII

I FIND AN UNEXPECTED FRIEND

GLEN bade Roper take the handkerchief from my mouth, and when that was done his creased face smiled at me over the lantern.

"About the *Royal Fortune?*" he said smoothly.

Peter Tortue nodded, and absently cleaned the blade of his knife upon the thighs of his breeches. There was no reply for me to make, and I waited.

"You were over to St. Mary's to-day?"

"Yes."

"What did you do there?"

"I bought a pair of silk stockings and some linen."

George Glen sniggered like a man that leaves off a serious conversation to laugh politely at a bad joke.

"But it's true," I cried.

"Did you speak of the *Royal Fortune?*"

"No," and, as luck would have it, I had not—not even to the Rev. Mr. Milray.

"Not to a living soul?"

"No."

"Did you go up to Star Castle?"

"No."

"Did you speak to Captain Hathaway?"

"No."

"'There's poor old George,' you said. 'Old George Glen,' says you, 'what was quartermaster with Cap'n Roberts on the *Royal*——'"

"No," I cried.

"Did you mention Peter Tortue?" said the Frenchman.

"No. Would you be sitting here if I had? There would be a company of soldiers scouring the island for you."

"That's reasonable," said Tortue, and the rest echoed his words. In a little there was silence. Tortue set to work again with his knife. It flashed backwards and forwards, red with the candle light as though it ran blood. It shone in my eyes and dazzled me, and somehow, there came back to me a recollection of that hot night in Clutterbuck's rooms when everything had glittered with an intolerable brightness, and Dick

I FIND AN UNEXPECTED FRIEND

Parmiter had been set upon the table to tell his story. I was vaguely wondering what they were all doing at this moment in London, Clutterbuck, Macfarlane, and the rest, when the questions began again.

"You came back from St. Mary's to New Grimsby?"

"Yes."

"Did you tell Parmiter?"

"No."

"From St. Mary's you crossed the island to Merchant's Point?"

"Yes."

"Did you tell the girl?"

Here a lie was obviously needful, and I did not scruple to tell it.

"No."

Peter Tortue leaned forward to me with a shrewd glance in his keen eyes.

"You are her lover," he said. "You told her."

I lifted my eyes from his knife, looked him in the eyes, and sustained his glance.

"I am not her lover," I said; "that is a damned lie."

He did not lose his temper, but repeated:

"You told her," and George Glen looked in again with his whole face screwed into a wink.

"You said to her, 'My dear,' says you, 'there's old George,'" and at that I lost my temper.

"I said nothing of the kind," I cried. "Am I a parrot that I cannot open my lips without old George popping out of them? But what's the use of talking. Do what you will, I have done. If I had betrayed your secret, do you think I should be walking home alone, and you upon the island? But I have done. I had a bargain to strike with you, I thought to find you all at the inn—but I have done."

To tell the truth, I had no longer any hope of life. Glen, for all his winks and smiles, would stop short of no cruelty. Peter Tortue quietly polished his knife upon his thigh. He was a big Brittany man, with shrewd eyes and an unchanging face. The rest squatted and stared curiously at me. The light of the lantern fell upon their callous faces, they were lookers-on at a show, of which perhaps, they had seen the like before, they were not concerned in this affair of the *Royal Fortune* nor how it ended.

"So you told no one."

"No one."

I FIND AN UNEXPECTED FRIEND

I closed my eyes and leaned back against the partition. I was utterly helpless in their hands, and I hoped they would be quick. I remember that I regretted very much I could send no word to the girl at Merchant's Rock, and that I was very glad she had not delayed her music till to-morrow night, but both regret and gladness were of a numbed and languid kind.

Then Glen asked me another question, and it spurred my will to alertness.

"How did you know that I was quartermaster on the *Royal Fortune*?"

I could not remind him that he had let the ship's name drop from his lips four years ago. It would be as much as to say that Helen had told me. It would confess that I had spoken with her of the *Royal Fortune*. Yet I must answer, and without the least show of hesitation. I caught at the first plausible reason which occurred to me. I said: "Cullen Mayle told me," and that answer saved my life. For Glen remarked, "Yes, he knew," and nodded to Tortue: Tortue lifted the knife in his hand, and again I closed my eyes. But the next thing I heard was a snap as the blade shut into the handle, and the next thing after that Tortue's voice deliberately speaking:

"George Glen, you never had the brains of a louse. You can smirk and wriggle, and you're handy with a weapon, but, you never had no brains."

I opened my eyes pretty wide at that, and I saw that the three younger faces were now kindled out of their sluggishness. It was that mention of Cullen Mayle which had wrought the change. These three took no particular interest in the *Royal Fortune*, but they had every interest in the doings of Cullen Mayle, and they now alertly followed all that Tortue said. George Glen leaned forward.

"Who's cap'en here, Peter Tortue?" said he. "Was you with us on the Sierra Leone River? Nat Roper there, Blads, you James Skyrm, speak up, lads, was he with us?"

"My son was," said Tortue calmly.

"And what sort of answer is that? 'Tis lucky for you Cap'en Roberts isn't aboard this shed. He wouldn't have understood that language, not he—and he wouldn't have troubled you for an explanation neither. Here's a fine thing, lads! If a man dies, his father, what's been lying in the lap of luxury at home, is to have his share. That's a nice new rule for gentlemen adventurers, and not

I FIND AN UNEXPECTED FRIEND

content with his share, wants to set up for cap'en. I have a good mind to learn you modesty, Peter, just as Roberts would have learnt you."

He was talking quite smoothly, with a grin all over his face, but I never saw a man that looked so dangerous. Peter Tortue, however, was in no way discomposed.

"Why, you blundering fool," he answered, "where would you ha' been but for me? No, I wasn't on the Sierra Leone River with you, or you wouldn't be eating your hearts and your pockets empty upon Tresco. No, I am not your captain, or you wouldn't never have lost track of Cullen Mayle at Wapping."

There were four faces now alertly watching Peter Tortue, and the fourth was mine. It was not merely that my life hung upon his predominance, but there was the best of chances now that I might get to the bottom of the mystery of their watching.

"You talk of Roberts," he continued, "well you're not the only man that knew Roberts, and would Roberts have let Cullen Mayle slip through his fingers—at Wapping too? Good Lord, it makes me sick to look at you, George Glen!" and he turned to Roper, "Who was it found the track for you; was it him or me?" he cried. "Who was it found the nigger and sailed from the port o' London to Penzance, ay, and would ha' found out the nigger's message if he hadn't had the sickness on him. Was it him or was it me? Why the nigger knowed you all! Would he ha' sailed to Penzance on that boat if he had seen a face on board that he had known? not he."

"That's true," said Roper.

"Who brought you all to Tresco, eh? Who hindered you from rushing the house, ay, hindered you in the face of your captain, and a deal you'ld ha' found if you had rushed the house. A lot he knows, your captain. P'raps he thought Adam Mayle was the man to leave a polite note on his mantelshelf, telling us where to look. Who told you to wait for Cullen Mayle?"

"We have waited," answered Glen. "How long are we to wait? Where is Cullen Mayle?"

Peter Tortue threw up his hands.

"No wonder you all dry in the sun at the end of it," he cried, "my word! We haven't got Cullen Mayle, but haven't we got the man as knows him? What's he doing at Tresco if he wasn't sent by Cullen Mayle who daren't show his face because we're here? Not worth my share,

I FIND AN UNEXPECTED FRIEND

ain't I? and you that can't add two and two! See here! Dick Parmiter goes to London, don't he? He goes after the nigger come; what for, but to find Cullen Mayle, and say as we're here? He knows where Cullen's to be found, and down comes the stranger here. And we ha' got him tucked up comfortable, and we know tricks that Roberts taught us to make him speak, don't we? And you want to jab a knife into him. You make me sick, George Glen—fair sick! Suppose you do jab a knife into him, and bury him here under the stones, do you think the girl 'll take it quite easy and natural? Or will you go down the hill and rush the house? And then if you please, what'll you all be doing to-morrow? Well, you are captain, George Glen, but what has your crew to say to this? Come! Am I to talk to Mr. Berkeley, or will you set your own course, and steer for execution dock?"

There was no hesitation in the answer. With one accord they leaned to Tortue's proposal.

I could not see that I was in a much better case. Tortue was to put to me questions, the very questions which I wished to ask, and I was expected to answer them. I should have to answer them if I was to come off with my life. The men sat hungrily about me awaiting my answers. It would not take them long to discover that I was tricking them, that I had no knowledge whatever about their concerns beyond that one dangerous item that Glen and Tortue had sailed on the *Royal Fortune*, and when that discovery was made, why, out of mere resentment they would let Glen have his way.

However, I was still alive, and the girl was still at Merchant's Point. These men were plainly growing impatient of their long stay upon the island; and once I was out of the way, who was to stand between them and the girl?

I summoned my wits together, and ran quickly over my mind what I did know. I had a few fresh hints from Tortue's arguments to add to my knowledge. I knew why they were watching for Cullen Mayle. He was to show them where to look for something. It was that something about which Glen had talked to Adam Mayle the night Cullen was driven away; Cullen had overheard, and he had gone out in search of it to the Sierra Leone River. Glen and his companions had done likewise. It was in some degree apparent now what that something was: namely, treasure of some sort from the *Royal Fortune*, and buried on

I FIND AN UNEXPECTED FRIEND 183

the banks of the Sierra Leone River. They had not found it, and their presence here, and certain words, told me why. Adam Mayle had been first with them.

So much I could venture to think of. For the rest I must wait upon the questions; and, fortunately for me, Glen was a man of much garrulity.

"You spoke of a bargain," said Tortue. "What do you propose?"

"Halves!" said I, as bold as brass.

There was an outcry against the proposal, and it mightily relieved me, for it proved to me I was right. It was treasure they were after, but of what kind? I had now to puzzle my brains over that. Was it specie? Hardly, I thought, for Adam Mayle would not have hidden money upon Tresco. Was it a treasure of jewels, then?

"Halves," said George Glen with a titter. "A very good proposal, Mr. Berkeley, by daylight, with a company of soldiers within call."

Jewels, I thought: yes, jewels—jewels that might be recognized, jewels that Adam Mayle would keep hidden to himself so long as there was no pressing need to dispose of them.

"As it is," continued Glen, "we take all, but we give you your life. That's a fair offer."

"Yes, that's fair," said Roper.

I hazarded it.

"Very well," said I. "You can find your jewels for yourselves."

I expected an explosion of wrath; I met with only mute surprise.

"Jewels!" said Roper at length.

"Well, isn't the cross thick with them?" said Tortue to Roper.

"It wouldn't be of much use to us without," sniggered Glen. "Lord, but that was a clever stroke of Roberts'—the cleverest thing he ever done. Right under the guns of the African Comp'ny's fort she lay in Sierra Leone harbour—a Portuguese ship of twenty guns. At a quarter to eleven there was her crew, as many as might be —we could hear 'em singing and laughing as we pulled across the water to 'em—and at ten minutes past three there wasn't a mother's son of them all alive; and no noise, mind you. Rich she was, too. Sugar—we had run short of sugar for our punch, and welcome it was—sugar, skins, tobacco, ninety thousand moidors, and this cross with the diamonds for the King of Portugal. Roberts himself said he had never seen stones like it, and he was a good judge of stones was Roberts. He

I FIND AN UNEXPECTED FRIEND 185

was quick, too. Why, we had that cross on the dinghy and were well up the Sierra Leone River before daybreak, just the three of us—Roberts, me, and Adam Mayle—Kennedy he called himself then, being a gentleman born and with more sense than the rest of us. He buried the cross, two days sail up the Sierra Leone River, and Roberts made a chart of its bearings. He gave it to me on the deck of the *Royal Fortune* when he was mortally wounded, and I kept it all the time we were in prison. I showed it to Adam Mayle when we escaped, but we had no means to get at it—at least, I hadn't. Adam, he was a gentleman born, and had got his savings placed all safe in his own name."

I hoped Glen would go on in this strain until my slip was forgotten. I was, besides, acquiring information. But Roper cut him short.

"It was a cross—it wasn't jewels," said he, suspiciously; and suddenly Tortue interrupted.

"'Halves' was what you said, I think," he remarked, rather quickly, and I could almost have believed that he was trying to cover up my mistake. I took advantage of his interruption as quickly as he had made it.

"Half for you, half for Cullen," said I; and

immediately Tortue flung out in an extravagant passion. He threatened me, he threatened Cullen, he opened his knife and gesticulated, he cursed, until I began to wonder: was he acting? Was this anger a pretence to divert attention finally from my unlucky guess? I could not be sure. I could conceive no reason for such a pretence. But certainly, whether he intended it or not, he brought about that result; for his companions began to fear he would make an end of me before they had got the information where the cross was hid, and so busied themselves with appeasing him. He permitted himself at the last to be appeased, and George Glen took up the argument.

"Look you here, Mr. Berkeley," said he, "we're reasonable men, and it's no more than fair you should be reasonable too, seeing as how you are uncomfortably placed. That was took up by Adam Mayle, and he never meant his son to finger it. 'A damned ungrateful, supercilious whelp,' says he to me in the lad's own bedroom; yes, in his own bedroom"—for, as may be imagined, I had started. Here was the explanation of how Cullen discovered George Glen's business. I hoisted myself up against the partition as well as I could. How I prayed that Glen would go

I FIND AN UNEXPECTED FRIEND

on! He was sufficiently garrulous, if only he was not interrupted, and he was arguing for all of them. "'A damned ungrateful, supercilious whelp,' he said; 'and George,' said he, as I read out the chart, 'I'd sooner let the cross rot to pieces in the Sierra Leone mud than fetch it home for him to have a share of. I've enough for myself and the girl. I'll not stir a finger,' says he, 'and if it was here now I'd have it buried with me.' Those were his very words, which he spoke to me not half an hour after he had driven Cullen from the house, and in the lad's own bedroom, where we couldn't be overheard."

"But you were overheard," said I, "Cullen Mayle overheard you." Glen jumped on to his feet, his mouth dropped, he stood staring at me in a daze, and then he thumped one fist down into the palm of the other.

"By God it's true," he said, "he was in the curtains."

"He was in bed," said I.

"By God it's true," repeated Glen, and he sat down again on the floor. "So that's how Cullen Mayle found out. I was mightily astonished to find him at Sierra Leone on the same business as ourselves. But it's true. I remember there was a noise, and I cried out, 'What's that?' with a sort of jump, and Adam he says, pleasant like, 'It's the hangman, George;' but it wasn't, it was Cullen Mayle."

I think that every one laughed as Glen ended, except myself. I could even at that moment, but be sensible what a strange picture it made; those two old ruffians sitting over against each other in the bedroom, and Cullen waked up from his sleep in bed to lie quiet and overhear them.

"So you see, it isn't reasonable Cullen should have half since his father never meant him to have any," he continued.

"But without Cullen you would get nothing at all," said I.

"Why not since we have you?"—and then I made a slip—I answered: "But Cullen Mayle told me where the cross is."

"But Cullen Mayle doesn't know," said Roper, "else would he have gone hunting to Sierra Leone for it?"

"Told him where to look for the plan, he means." Tortue interrupted again. This time I could not mistake. He glanced at me with too much significance. For some reason, he was standing my friend.

I FIND AN UNEXPECTED FRIEND

"Of course," said I, "where to look for the plan."

So it was a plan they needed, a plan of the spot where Adam Mayle had buried the cross. Where could that plan be, in what unlikely place would Adam have hid it?

I ran over my mind the rooms, and the furniture of the house. There was no bureau, no secretaire. But I had to make up my mind. This last slip had awakened my captor's suspicions. The faces about me menaced me.

"Well, where is the plan?"

I thought over all that Glen had said to-night—was a clue to be got there?

"I haven't it," said I, to gain time.

"But where are we to look for it?" again asked Roper, and he put his hand in his coat-pocket.

"Speak up," said Tortue, and I read his meaning in the glance of his eyes. He meant—"Name some spot, any spot!" But I knew! It had come upon me like an inspiration, I had no shadow of doubt where that plan was. I said:

"Where are you to look for the plan? Glen has told you. Adam Mayle would rather have had the cross buried with him than that Cullen should have it. He couldn't have the treasure buried with him, but he could and did the plan. Look in Adam Mayle's grave. You will find a stick with a brass handle to it—a sword stick, but the sword's broken off short. In the hollow of that stick you'll find the plan." Tortue nodded at me with approval. The rest jumped up from the ground.

"We have time to-night," said Roper, and stretching out a hand he pulled my watch from my fob. "It is eleven o'clock," and he put the watch in his own pocket. "Where's Adam Mayle buried?" asked another.

"In the Abbey Grounds," said I.

"But we want spades," objected Tortue, "we want a pick."

"They are here," said Glen, with an evil smile, "we had them ready," and he grinned at me. "Mr. Berkeley comes with us, I think," said he smoothly, "untie his legs."

"Yes," said Roper with an oath. He was in a heat of excitement. "And if he has told us wrong, good God, we'll bury him with Adam Mayle."

But I had no doubt that I was right. I remembered what Clutterbuck had told me of Adam's vindictiveness. He would hide that plan if he

I FIND AN UNEXPECTED FRIEND 191

could, and he could have chosen no surer place. No doubt he would have destroyed that plan when he knew that he was dying, but he was struck down with paralysis, and could not stir a finger. He could only order the stick to be buried with him.

They unfastened my legs. Roper blew out the lantern, and we went out of the shed, on to the hillside. Glen despatched Blads upon some errand, and the man hurried up the hill towards New Grimsby. Glen leisurely walked along the the slope of the hill. I followed him, and the rest behind me. The moon had gone down, and the night, though clear enough, was dark. We walked on for about five minutes, until some one treading close upon my heels suddenly tripped me up. My hands were still tied behind my back, so that I could not save myself from a fall. But Tortue picked me up, and as he did so whispered in my ear:

"Is the plan there?"

I answered, "Yes."

I would have staked my life upon it; in fact, I was staking my life upon it.

CHAPTER XIII

IN THE ABBEY GROUNDS

WE kept along the ridge of hill towards the east of the island, and met no one, nor, indeed, were we likely to do. I could look down on either side to the sea. I saw the cottages on the shore of New Grimsby harbour on the one side, and on the other the house at Merchant's Point, and the half-dozen houses scattered on the grass at Old Grimsby, that went by the name of Dolphin Town, and nowhere was there a twinkle of light.

Tresco was in bed.

We descended a little to our left, and rounded the shoulder of the hill at the eastern end of the island, through a desolate moorland of gorse; but once we had rounded the shoulder, we were in an instant amongst trees of luxuriant foliage, and in a hollow sheltered from the winds. The Abbey ruins stood up from a small plateau in the bosom of the trees, its broken arches and columns showing very dismal against the sky, and everywhere fragments of crumbling wall cropped up unexpected through the grass.

The burial ground was close to an eel pond, which glimmered below, nearer to the sea, and a path overgrown with weeds wound downwards to the graves.

I could not tell in which corner Adam Mayle was buried, so Roper was sent forward with the lantern to look amongst the headstones. For half an hour he searched; the flame of the candle danced from grave to grave as though it were the restless soul of some sinner buried there. The men who remained with me grew impatient, for opposite to us, across the road, lay St. Mary's and the harbour of Hugh Town; and on this clear night the speck of light in the Abbey grounds would be visible at a great distance. I was beginning to wonder whether Adam had a headstone at all to mark his resting-place, when a cry came upwards to our ears and the lantern was swung aloft in the air.

One loud, unanimous shout answered that cry.

"Come," shouted Glen, and seizing hold of the end of the rope where it went round my chest, he began to run down the path. The others jostled and tumbled after him in an extreme excitement. All discretion was tossed to the winds. They laughed, shouted, and leaped while they ran as though they already had the cross in their keeping. What with Glen tugging at the end in front and the others pushing and thrusting at me from behind, it was more than I could do to keep my feet. Twice I fell forward on my knees and brought them to a stop. Glen turned upon me in a fury.

"Loose his hands then, George," said Tortue.

"No," returned George, with an oath, and he plucked on the rope until somehow I stumbled on to my feet, and we all set to running again.

Things were taking on an ugly look for me. Those men were growing ten times more savage since the grave had been discovered; they were in a heat of excitement. In their movements, in their faces, in their words, a violent ferocity was evident. They had made their bargain with me, but would they keep it once they had the plan in their hands? I had no doubt their arrangements were made for an instant departure from the islands. One could not be a day upon Tresco without hearing some hint of the luggers which did a great smuggling trade between Scilly and the port of Roscoff in Brittany. No doubt Glen and Tortue had made their account with one of these to carry them into France. I was the more sure of this when Blads returned. I could not but think he had been sent so that a boat might be ready, and it seemed unlikely they would leave me alive behind them when the mere scruple of a bargain only held their hands.

We were now come to the grave. It had a headstone but no slab to cover it; only a boulder from the seashore by which Adam had lived was with a pretty fancy imposed upon the mound.

Roper hung the lantern on to a knob of the headstone; and already Glen had snatched the pick and thrust it under the boulder. It needed but one heave upon the pick, and the boulder tottered and rolled from the grave with a crash. It stopped quite close to my feet. I looked at it, then I looked at the grave, and from the grave to the sailors. But they had noticed nothing; they were already digging furiously at the grave. In their excitement they had noticed nothing; even Tortue was kneeling in the lantern-light watching the gleam of the spades, sensible of nothing but that each shovelful cast up on the side brought them by a shovelful nearer to their prize. And they dug with such furious speed, taking each his turn, each anticipating his turn! For before one man had stepped, dripping with sweat from the trench, another had leaped in, and the spade fell from one man's grasp into the palm of another. Once a spade jarred upon a piece of rock, and the man who drove it into the earth cursed. I had a sudden flutter of hope that the spade was broken, and that by so much the issue would be delayed, but the digger resumed his work. I looked over to St. Mary's, but the town was quiet; one light gleamed, it was only the light at the head of the jetty. And even in Tresco such infinitesimal chance of interruption as there had ever been had disappeared. For the men had ceased even from their oaths. There was not even a whisper to be shared amongst them; there was no sound but the laboured sound of their breathing. They worked in silence.

I had no longer any hope. I saw now and again Roper, as he slapped down a spadeful of earth beside me, look with a grim significant smile at me, and perhaps his fellow would catch the look and imitate it. I noticed that George Glen, as he took down the lantern from time to time and held it over the trench, would flash it towards me; and he, too, would smile and perhaps wink at Roper in the trench. The winks and smiles were easy as print to read. They were agreeing between themselves: the unspoken word was going round; they did not mean to keep their part of the bargain, and when they left the Abbey grounds the mound upon Adam's grave would be a foot higher than when they entered them.

But this unspoken understanding had no longer any power to frighten me. I tried to catch Peter Tortue's attention; I shuffled a foot upon the ground; but he paid no heed. He was on all fours by the grave-side peering into the trench, and I dared not call to him. I wanted to contradict what I had said outside the shed upon the hillside. I wanted to whisper to him:

"The plan you search for is not there."

If they were meaning to break their part of the bargain it mattered very little, for I was unable to keep mine.

I had suspected that from the moment the boulder was uprooted; I knew it a moment after the lantern was hung upon the headstone. The stone had rested on that grave for two years, yet at the fresh pressure of the pick it had given and swayed and rolled from its green pedestal. It had tumbled at my feet, and there was not even a clot of earth or a pebble clinging to it. Moreover, on the grave itself there was grass where it had rested. For all its weight, it had not settled into the ground or so much as worn the herbage. Yet it had rested there two years!

The lantern was hung upon the headstone, and its light showed to me that close to the ground the headstone had been chipped. It was as though some one had swung a pick and by mistake had struck the edge of the headstone. Moreover, whoever had swung the pick had swung it recently. For whereas the face of the granite was dull and weatherbeaten, this chipped edge sparkled like quartz.

The aspect of the grave itself confirmed me. Some pains had been taken to replace the sods of grass upon the top, but all about the mound, wherever the lantern-light fell, I could see lumps of fresh clay.

The grave had been opened, and recently—I did not stop then to consider by whom—and secretly. It could have been opened but for the one reason. There would be no plan there for Glen to find.

Roper uttered an exclamation and stopped digging. His spade had struck something hard. Glen lowered the lantern into the trench, and the light struck up on to his face and the face of the diggers.

I hazarded a whisper to Tortue, and certainly no one else heard it, but neither did Tortue. Roper struck his spade in with renewed vigour, and a stifled cry which burst at the same moment from the five mouths told me the coffin-lid was disclosed. I whispered again the louder:

"Tortue! Tortue!" and with no better result.

The pick was handed down at Roper's call. I *spoke* now, and at last he heard. He turned his head across his shoulder towards me, but he only motioned me to silence. The pick rang upon wood, and now I called:

"Tortue! Tortue!"

Still no one but Tortue heard. This time, however, he rose from his knees and came to me. Glen looked up for an instant.

"See that he is fast!" he said, and so looked back into the grave.

"What is it?" asked Tortue.

"The plan has gone. Loose my hands!"

I could no longer see Roper; he had stooped down below the lip of the trench.

"Gone!" said Tortue. "How?"

"Some one has been here before you, but within this last week, I'll swear. Loose my hands."

"Some one!" he exclaimed savagely. "Who? who?" and he shook me by the arms.

"I do not know."

"Swear it."

"I do. Loose my hands."

"Remember it is I who save you."

His knife was already out of his pocket; he had already muffled it in his coat and opened it; he was making a pretence to see whether the end was still fast. I could feel the cold blade between the rope and my wrist, when, with a shout, Roper stood erect, the stick in one hand, a sheet of paper flourishing in the other.

He drew himself out of the trench and spread the paper out on a pile of clay at the graveside. Glen held his lantern close to it. There were four streaming faces bent over that paper. I felt a tug at my wrists and the cord slacken as the knife cut through it.

"Take the rope with you," whispered Tortue.

The next moment there were five faces bent over that paper.

"On St. Helen's Island," cried Glen.

"Let me see!" exclaimed Tortue, leaning over his shoulder. "Three—what's that?—chains. Three chains east by the compass of the east window in the south aisle of the church."

And that was the last I heard. I stepped softly back into the darkness for a few paces, and then I ran at the top of my speed westwards towards New Grimsby, freeing my arms from the rope as I ran. Once I turned to look back. They were still gathered about that plan; their faces, now grown small, were clustered under the light of the lantern, and Tortue, with his flashing knife-blade, was pointing out upon the paper the position of the treasure. Ten minutes later I was well up the top of the hill. I saw a lugger steal round the point from New Grimsby and creep up in the shadow towards the Abbey grounds.

I spent that night in the gorse high up on the Castle Down. I had no mind to be caught in a trap at the Palace Inn.

From the top of the down, about an hour later, I saw the lugger come round the Lizard Point of Tresco and beat across to St. Helen's. As the day broke she pushed out from St. Helen's, and reaching past the Golden Ball into the open sea, put her tiller up and ran by the islands to the south.

There was no longer any need for me to hide among the gorse. I went down to the Palace Inn. No one was as yet astir, and the door, of course, was unlocked. I crept quietly up to my room and went to bed.

CHAPTER XIV

IN WHICH PETER TORTUE EXPLAINS HIS INTERVENTION ON MY BEHALF

As will be readily understood, when I woke up the next morning I was sensible at once of a great relief. My anxieties and misadventures of last night were well paid for after all. I could look at my swollen wrists and say that without any hesitation, the watchers had departed from their watching, and what if they had carried away the King of Portugal's great jewelled cross? Helen Mayle had no need of it, indeed, her great regret now was that she could not get rid of what she had; and as for Cullen, to tell the truth, I did not care a snap of the fingers whether he found a fortune or must set to work to make one. Other men had been compelled to do it—better men too, deuce take him! We were well quit of George Glen and his gang, though the price of the quittance was heavy. I would get up at once, run across to Merchant's Point, and tell Helen

Mayle——— My plans came to a sudden stop. Tell Helen Mayle precisely what? That Adam Mayle's grave had been rifled?

I lay staring up at the ceiling as I debated that question, and suddenly it slipped from my mind. That grave had been rifled before, and quite recently. I was as certain of that in the sober light of the morning as I had been during the excitement of last night. Why? It was not for the chart of the treasure, since the chart had been left. And by whom? So after all, here was I, who had waked up in the best of spirits too, with the world grown comfortable, confronted with questions as perplexing as a man could wish for. It was, as Cullen Mayle had said, at the inn near Axminster, most discouraging. And I turned over in bed and tried to go to sleep, that I might drive them from my mind. I should have succeeded too, but just as I was in a doze there came a loud rapping at the door, and Dick Parmiter danced into the room.

"They are gone, Mr. Berkeley," he cried.

"I know," I grumbled; "I saw them go," and stretched out my arms and yawned.

"Why, you have hurt your wrist," Dick exclaimed.

"No," said I, "it was George Glen's shake of the hand."

"They are gone," repeated Dick, gleefully, "all of them except Peter Tortue."

"What's that?" I cried, sitting up in the bed.

"All of them except Peter Tortue."

"To be sure," said I, scratching my head.

Now what in the world had Peter Tortue remained behind for? For no harm, that was evident, since I owed my life to his good offices last night. I was to remember that it was he who saved me. I was, then, to make some return. But what return?"

I threw my pillow at Parmiter's head.

"Deuce take you, Dicky! My bed was not such a plaguey restful place before that it needed you to rumple it further. Well, since I mayn't sleep late i' the morning like a gentleman, I'll get up."

I tried to put together some sort of plausible explanation which would serve for Helen Mayle while I was dressing. But I could not hit upon one, and besides Parmiter made such a to-do over brushing my clothes this morning that that alone was enough to drive all reasoning out of one's head.

"Dick," said I as he handed me my coat, "you

have had, if my memory serves me, some experience of womenfolk."

Dick nodded his head in a mournful fashion.

"Mother!" said he.

"Precisely," said I. "Now, here's a delicate question. Do you always tell womenfolk the truth?"

"No," said he, stoutly.

"Do you tell them—shall we say quibbles,— then?"

"Quibbles?" said Dick, opening his mouth.

"It is not a fruit, Dicky," said I, "so you need not keep it open. By quibbles I mean lies. Do you tell your womenfolk lies, when the truth is not good for them to know?"

"No," said Dick, as steadily as before, "for they finds you out."

"Precisely," I agreed. "But since you neither tell the truth nor tell lies, what in the world do you do?"

"Well," answered Dick, "I say that it's a secret which mother isn't to know for a couple of days."

"I see. And when the couple of days has gone?"

"Then mother has forgotten all about the secret."

I reflected for a moment or two.

" Dick."

" Yes."

" Did you ever try that plan with Miss Helen ? "

" No," said he, shaking his head.

" I will," said I, airily, " or something like it."

" Something like it would be best," said Dick.

The story which I told to Helen was not after all very like it. I said:

" The watchers have gone and gone for ever. They were here not for any revenge, but for their profit. There was a treasure in St. Helen's which Cullen Mayle was to show them the way to—if they could catch him and force him. They had some claim to it—I showed them the way."

" You ? " she exclaimed. " How ? "

" That I cannot tell you," said I. " I would beg you not to ask, but to let my silence content you. I could not tell you the truth and I do not think that I could invent a story to suit the occasion which would not ring false. The consequence is the one thing which concerns us, and there is no doubt of it. The watchers did not watch for an opportunity of revenge and they are gone."

"Very well," she said. "I was right after all, you see. The hand stretched out of the dark has done this service. For it is your doing that they are gone?"

I did not answer and she laughed a little and continued, "But I will not ask you. I will make shift to be content with your silence. Did Dick Parmiter come with you this morning?"

"Yes," I answered with a laugh, "but he was not with me last night."

Helen laughed again.

"Ah," she cried! "So it was your doing, and I have not asked you." Then she grew serious of a sudden. "But since they are gone"—she exclaimed, in a minute, her whole face alight with her thought—"since they are gone, Cullen may come and come in safety."

"Oh! yes, Cullen may come," I answered, perhaps a trifle roughly. "Cullen will be safe and may come. Indeed, I wonder that he was not here before this. He stole my horse upon the road and yet could not reach here first. I trudged a-foot, Cullen bestrode my horse and yet Tresco still pines for him. It is very strange unless he has a keen nose for danger."

My behaviour very likely was not the politest

imaginable, but then Helen's was no better. For although she displayed no anger at my rough words—I should not have cared a scrape of her wheezy fiddle if she had, but she did not, she merely laughed in my face with every appearance of enjoyment. I drew myself up very stiff. Here were all the limits of courtesy clearly over-stepped, but I at all events would not follow her example, nor allow her one glimpse of any exasperation which I might properly feel.

"Shall I go out and search for him in the highways and hedges?" I asked with severity.

"It would be magnanimous," said she biting her lip, and then her manner changed. "He rode your horse," she cried, "and yet he has fallen behind. He will be hurt then! Some accident has befallen him!"

"Or he has wagered my horse at some roadside inn and lost! It was a good horse, too."

She caught hold of my arm in some agitation.

"Oh! be serious!" she prayed.

"Serious quotha!" said I, drawing away from her hand with much dignity. "Let me assure you, madam, that the loss of a horse is a very serious affair, that the stealing of a horse is a very serious affair——"

"Well, well, I will buy it from you, saddle and stirrup and all," she interrupted.

"Madam," said I, when I could get my speech. "There is no more to be said."

"Heaven be praised!" said she. "And now it may be, you will condescend to listen to me. What am I to do? Suppose that he is hurt! Suppose that he is in trouble! Suppose that he still waits for my answer to his message! Suppose in a word that he does not come! What can I do? He may go hungering for a meal."

I did not think the contingency probable, but Helen was now speaking with so much sincerity of distress that I could not say as much.

"Unless he comes to Tresco I am powerless. It is true I have bequeathed everything to him, but then I am young," she said, with a most melancholy look in her big dark eyes. "Neither am I sickly."

"I will go back along the road and search for him," and this I spoke with sincerity. She looked at me curiously.

"Will you do that?" she asked in a doubtful voice, as though she did not know whether to be pleased or sorry.

"Yes," said I, and a servant knocked at the

door, and told me Parmiter wished to speak with me. I found the lad on the steps of the porch, and we walked down to the beach.

"What is it?" I asked.

"The Frenchman," said he, with a frightened air.

"Peter Tortue?"

"Yes."

I led him further along the beach lest any of the windows of the house should be open towards us, and any one by the open window.

"Where is he?"

Dick pointed up the hill.

"At the shed?" I asked.

"Yes. He was lying in wait on the hillside, and ran down when he saw that I was alone. He stays in the shed for you, and you are to go to him alone."

"Amongst the dead sailor-men?" said I, with a laugh. But the words were little short of blasphemy to Dick Parmiter. "Well, I was there last night, and no harm came to me."

"You were there last night?" cried Dick. "Then you will not go?"

"But I will," said I. "I am curious to hear what Tortue has to say to me. You may take my word for it, Dick, there's no harm in Peter Tortue. I shall be back within the hour. Hush! not a word of this!" for I saw Helen Mayle coming from the house towards us. I told her that I was called away, and would return.

"Do you take Dick with you?" she asked, with too much indifference. She held a big hat of straw by the ribbons and swung it to and fro. She did that also with too much indifference.

"No," said I, "I leave him behind. Make of him what you can. He cannot tell what he does not know."

The sum of Dick's knowledge, I thought, amounted to no more than this—that I had last night visited the shed, in spite of the dead sailor-men. I forgot for the moment that he was in my bedroom when I rose that morning.

The door of the shed was fastened on the inside; I rapped with my knuckles, and Tortue's voice asked who was there. When I told him, he unbarred the door.

"There is no one behind you?" said he, peering over my shoulder.

"Nay! Do you fear that I have brought the constables to take you? You may live in Tresco till you die if you will. What! Should I betray you, whose life you saved only last night?"

Peter opened the door wide.

"A night!" said he, with a shrug of the shoulders. "One can forget more than that in a night, if one is so minded."

I followed him into the shed. Here and there, through the chinks in the boards, a gleam of light slipped through. Outside it was noonday, within it was a sombre evening. I passed through the door of the partition into the inner room. The rafters above were lost in darkness, and before my eyes were accustomed to the gloom I stumbled over a slab of stone which had been lifted from its place in the floor. I turned to Tortue, who was just behind me, and he nodded in answer to my unspoken question. The spade and the pick had stood in that corner to the left, and this slab of stone had been removed in readiness. The darkness of the shed struck cold upon me all at once, as I thought of why that slab had been removed. I looked about me much as a man may look about his bedroom the day after he has been saved from his grave by the surgeon's knife. Everything stands as it did yesterday—this chair in this corner, that table just upon that pattern of the carpet, but it is all very strange and unfamiliar. It was against that board in the partition that I leaned my back; there sat George Glen with his evil smile, here Tortue polished his knife.

"Let us go out into the sunlight, for God's sake!" said I, and my foot struck against a piece of iron, which went tinkling across the stone floor. I picked it up. "They are gone," said I, with a shiver, "and there's an end of them. But this shed is a nightmarish sort of place for me. For God's sake, let us get into the sun!"

"Yes, they are gone," said Tortue, "but they would have stayed if they dared, if I hadn't set you free, for they went without the cross."

I was still holding that piece of iron in my hand. By the feel of it, it was a key, and I slipped it into my pocket quite unconsciously, for Tortue's words took me aback with surprise.

"Without the jewelled cross? But you had the plan," said I, as I stepped into the open. "I heard you describe the spot—three chains in a line east of the east window in the south aisle of the church."

"There was no trace of the cross."

"It was true then!" I exclaimed. "I was

sure of it, even after Roper had found the stick and the plan. It was true—that grave had been rifled before."

"Why should the plan have been put back, then?"

"God knows! I don't."

"Besides, if the grave had been rifled, the spot of ground on St. Helen's Island had not. There had been no spade at work there."

"Are you sure of that?"

"Yes."

"And you followed out the directions?"

"To the letter. Three chains east by the compass of the eastern window in the south aisle of St. Helen's Church, and four feet deep! We dug five and six feet deep. There was nothing, nor had the ground been disturbed."

"I cannot understand it. Why should Adam Mayle have been at such pains to hide the plan? Was it a grim joke to be played on Cullen?"

There was no means of answering the problem, and I set it aside.

"After all, they are gone," said I. "That is the main thing."

"All except me," said Tortue.

"Yes. Why have you stayed?"

Tortue threw himself on the ground and chewed at a stalk of grass.

"I saved your life last night," said he.

"I know. Why did you do it? Why did you cover my mistakes in that shed? Why did you cut the rope?"

"Because you could serve my turn. The cross!" he exclaimed, with a flourish. "I do not want the cross." He looked at me steadily for an instant with his shrewd eyes. "I want a man to nail on the cross, and you can help me to him. Where is Cullen Mayle?"

The words startled me all the more because there was no violence in the voice which spoke them—only a cold, deliberate resolution. I was never more thankful for the gift of ignorance than upon this occasion. I could assure him quite honestly,

"I do not know."

"But last night you knew."

"I spoke of many things last night of which I had no knowledge—the cross, the plan——"

"You knew where the plan was. Flesh! but you knew that!"

"I guessed."

"Guess, then, where Cullen Mayle is, and I'll be content."

"I have no hint to prompt a guess."

Tortue gave no sign of anger at my answer. He sat upon the grass, and looked with a certain sadness at the shed.

"It does not, after all, take much more than a night to forget," said he.

"I am telling you the truth, Tortue," said I, earnestly. "I do not know. I never met Cullen Mayle but once, and that was at a roadside inn. He stole my horse upon that occasion, so that I have no reason to bear him any goodwill."

"But because of him you came down to Tresco?" said Tortue quickly.

"No."

Tortue looked at me doubtfully. Then he looked at the house, and

"Ah! It was because of the girl."

"No! No!" I answered vehemently. I could not explain to him why I had come, and fortunately he did not ask for an explanation. He just nodded his head, and stood up without another word.

"I do not forget," said I pointing to the shed. "And if you should be in any need——" But I got no further in my offer of help; for he turned upon me suddenly, and anger at last had got the upper hand with him.

"Money, is it not?" he cried, staring down at me with his eyes ablaze. "Ay, that's the way with gentlefolk! You would give me as much as a guinea no doubt—a whole round gold guinea. Yes, I am in need," and with a violent movement he clasped his hands together. "Virgin Mary, but I am in need of Cullen Mayle, and you offer me a guinea!" and then hunching his shoulders he strode off over the hill.

So Helen Mayle's instinct was right. Out of the five men there was one who waited for Cullen's coming with another object than to secure the diamond cross. Would he continue to wait? I could not doubt that he would, when I thought upon his last vehement burst of passion. Tortue would wait upon Tresco, until, if Cullen did not come himself, some word of Cullen's whereabouts dropped upon his ear. It was still urgent, therefore, that Cullen Mayle should be warned, and if I was to go away in search of him, Helen must be warned too.

I walked back again towards Merchant's Point with this ill news heavy upon my mind, and as I came over the lip of the hollow, I saw Helen waiting by the gate in the palisade. She saw me at the same moment, and came up towards me at a run.

"Is there more ill-news?" I asked myself. "Or has Cullen Mayle returned?" and I ran quickly down to her.

"Has he come?" I asked, for she came to a stop in front of me with her face white and scared.

"Who?" said she absently, as she looked me over.

"Cullen Mayle," I answered.

"Oh, Cullen," she said, and it struck me as curious that this was the first time I had heard her speak his name with indifference.

"Because he must not show himself here. There is a reason! There is a danger still!"

"A danger," she said, in a loud cry, and then "Oh! I shall never forgive myself!"

"For what?"

She caught hold of my arm.

"See?" she said. "Your coat-sleeve is frayed. It was a rope did that last night. No use to deny it. Dick told me. He saw that a rope too had seared your wrists. Tell me! What happened last night? I must know!"

"You promised not to ask," said I, moving away from her.

"Well, I break my promise," said she. "But I must know," and she turned and kept pace with me, down the hill, through the house into the garden. During that time she pleaded for an answer in an extreme agitation, and I confess that her agitation was a sweet flattery to me. I was inclined to make the most of it, for I could not tell how she would regard the story of my night's adventures. It was I after all who caused old Adam Mayle's bones to be disturbed; and I understood that it was really on that account that I had shrunk from telling her. She had a right to know, no doubt. Besides there was this new predicament of Tortue's stay. I determined to make a clean breast of the matter. She listened very quietly without an exclamation or a shudder; only her face lost even the little colour which it had, and a look of horror widened in her eyes. I told her of my capture on the hillside, of Tortue's intervention, of the Cross and the stick in the coffin. I drew a breath and described that scene in the Abbey grounds, and how I escaped; and still she said no word and gave no sign. I told her of their futile search upon St. Helen's, and how I had witnessed their departure from the top of the Castle Down. Still she walked by my side silent, and wrapped in horror. I faltered through this last incident of Tortue's stay and came to a lame finish, amongst the trees at the end of the garden. We turned and walked the length of the garden to the house.

"I know," I said. "When I guessed the stick held the plan, I should have held my tongue. But I did not think of that. It was not easy to think at all just at that time, and I must needs be quick. They spoke of attacking the house, and I dreaded that. . . . I should not have been able to give you any warning. . . . I should not have been able to give you any help . . . . for, you see, the slab of stone was already removed in the shed."

"Oh, don't!" she cried out, and pressed her hands to her temples. "I shall never forgive myself. Think! A week ago you and I were strangers. It cannot be right that you should go in deadly peril because of me."

"Madam," said I, greatly relieved, "you make too much of a thing of no great consequence. I hope to wear my life lightly."

"Always?" said she quickly, as she stopped and looked at me.

I stopped, too, and looked at her.

"I think so," said I, but without the same confidence. "Always."

She had a disconcerting habit of laughing when there was no occasion whatever for laughter. She fell into that habit now, and I hastened to recall her to Tortue's embarrassing presence on the island.

"Of course," said I, "a word to the Governor at Star Castle and we are rid of him. But he stood between me and my death, and he trusts to my silence."

"We must keep that silence," she answered.

"Yet he waits for Cullen Mayle, and—it will not be well if those two men meet."

"Why does he wait? Do you know that, too?"

I did not know, as I told her, though I had my opinion, of which I did not tell her.

"The great comfort is this. Tortue did not make one upon that expedition to the Sierra Leone River, but his son did. Tortue only fell in with George Glen and his gang at an ale-house in Wapping, and *after*—that is the point—after Glen had lost track of Cullen Mayle. Tortue, therefore, has never seen Cullen, does not know him. We have an advantage there. So should he come to Tresco, while I go back along the road to search for him, you must make your profit of that advantage."

She stopped again.

"You will go, then?"

"Why, yes."

She shook her head, reflectively.

"It is not right," she said.

"I am going chiefly," said I, "because I wish to recover my horse."

She always laughed when I mentioned that horse, and her laughter always made me angry.

"Do you doubt I have a horse?" I asked. "Or rather *had* a horse? Because Cullen Mayle stole it, stole it deliberately from under my nose—a very valuable horse which I prized even beyond its value—and he stole it."

The girl was in no way impressed by my wrath, and she said, pleasantly:

"I am glad you said that. I am glad to know that with it all, you are mean like other men."

"Madam," I returned, "when Cullen Mayle stole my horse, and rode away upon it, he put out his tongue at me. I made no answer. Nor do I make any answer to the remark which you have this moment addressed to me."

"Oh, sir!" said she, "here are fine words, and here's a curtsey to match them;" and spreading out her frock with each hand, she sank elaborately to the very ground.

We walked for some while longer in the garden, without speech, and the girl's impertinence gradually slipped out of my mind. The sea murmured lazily upon the other side of the hedge, and I had full in view St. Helen's Island and the ruined church upon its summit. The south aisle of the church pointed towards the house, and through the tracery of a rude window I could see the sky.

"I wonder who in the world can have visited the Abbey burial-ground and rifled that grave?"

The question perplexed me more and more, and I wondered whether Helen could throw light upon it. So I asked her, but she bent her brows in a frown, and in a little she answered:

"No, I can think of no one."

I held out my hand to her. "This is good-bye," said I.

"You go to-day?" she asked, but did not take my hand.

"Yes, if I can find a ship to take me. I go to

St. Helen's first. Can I borrow your boat; Dick will bring it back. I want to see that east window in the aisle."

A few more words were said, and I promised to return, whether I found Cullen Mayle or not. And I did return, but sooner than I expected, for I returned that afternoon.

CHAPTER XV

THE LOST KEY IS FOUND

IT happened in this way. I took Dick Parmiter with me and sailed across to St. Helen's. We beached the boat on the sand near to the well and quarantine hut, and climbed up eastwards till we came to the hole which Glen's party had dug. The ground sloped away from the church in this direction; and as I stood on the edge of the hole with my face towards the side of the aisle, I could just see over the grass the broken cusp of the window. It was exactly opposite to me.

It occurred to me, however, that Glen had measured the distance wrong. So I sent Dick in the boat across to Tresco to borrow a measure, and while he was away I examined the ground there around; but it was all covered with grass and bracken, which evidently had not been disturbed. Here and there were bushes of brambles, but, as I was at pains to discover, no search for the cross had been made beneath them.

In the midst of my search Dick came back to me with a tape measure, and we set to work from the window of the church. The measure was for a few yards, so that when we had run it out to its full length, keeping ever in the straight line, it was necessary to fix some sort of mark in the ground, and start afresh from that; and for a mark I used a big iron key which I had in my pocket. Three chains brought us exactly to the hole which had been dug, and holding the key in my hand, I said:

"They made no mistake. It is plain the plan was carelessly drawn."

And Dick said to me: "That's the key of our cottage."

I handed it to him to make sure. He turned it over in his hand.

"Yes," said he, "that's the key;" and he added reproachfully, with no doubt a lively recollection of his mother's objurgations: "So you had it all the time."

"I found it this morning, Dick," said I.

"Where?"

"In the shed on the Castle Down. Now, how the deuce did it get there? The dead sailormen had no use for keys."

"It's very curious," said Dick.

"Very curious and freakish," said I, and I sat down on the grass to think the matter out.

"Let me see, your mother missed it in the morning after I came to Tresco."

"That's three days ago." And I could hardly believe the boy. It seemed to me that months had passed. But he was right.

"Yes, three days ago. Your mother missed it in the morning. It is likely, then, that it was taken from the lock of the door the night before."

"That would be the night," said Dick, suspiciously, "when you tapped on my window."

"The night, in fact, when I first landed on Tresco. Wait a little."

Dick sat still upon the grass, and I took the key from his hand into mine. There were many questions which at that moment perplexed me—that hideous experience in Cullen Mayle's bedroom, the rifling of Adam Mayle's grave, the replacing of the plan in it and the disappearance of the cross, and I was in that state of mind when everything new and at all strange presented itself as a possible clue to the mystery. It seemed to me that the key which I held was very much more than a mere rusty iron key of a door that was never locked. I felt that it was the key to the door of the mystery which baffled me, and that feeling increased in me into a solid conviction as I held it in my hand. I seemed to see the door opening, and opening very slowly. The chamber beyond the door was dark, but my eyes would grow accustomed to the darkness if only I did not turn them aside. As it was, even now I began to see dim, shadowy things which, uncomprehended though they were, struck something of a thrill into my blood, and something of a chill, too.

"The night that I landed upon Tresco," I said, "we crossed the Castle Down, I nearly fell on to the roof of the shed, where all the dead sailormen were screeching in unison."

"Yes!" said Dick, in a low voice, and I too looked around me to see that we were not overheard. Dick moved a little nearer to me with an uneasy working of his shoulders.

"Do you remember the woman who passed us?" I asked.

"You said it was a woman."

"And it was."

I had the best of reasons to be positive upon, that point. I had scratched my hand in the gorse and I had seen the blood of my scratches the next day on the dress of the woman who had brushed against me as she passed. That woman was Helen Mayle. Had she come from the shed? What did she need with the key?

"Is that shed ever used?" I asked.

"Not now."

"Whom does it belong to?"

He nodded over towards Merchant's Rock.

"Then Adam Mayle used it?"

"Cullen Mayle used it."

"Cullen!"

I sprang up to my feet and walked away; and walked back; and walked away again. The shadowy things were indeed becoming visible; my eyes were growing indeed accustomed to the darkness; and, indeed, the door was opening. Should I close, slam it to, lock it again and never open it? For I was afraid.

But if I did shut it and lock it I should come back to it perpetually, I should be perpetually fingering the lock. No; I would open the door wide and see what was within the room. I came back to Dick.

"What did Cullen Mayle use it for?"

"He was in league with the Brittany smugglers.

Brandy, wine, and lace were landed on the beach of a night and carried up to the shed."

"Were they safe there?"

Dick laughed. Here he was upon firm ground, and he answered with some pride:

"When Cullen Mayle lived here, the collector of customs daren't for his life have landed on Tresco in daylight."

"And at night the dead sailormen kept watch."

"There wasn't a man who would go near the shed."

"So Cullen Mayle would not have needed a key to lock the shed?"

"No, indeed!" and another laugh.

"Could he have needed a key for any other purpose? Dick, we will go slowly, very slowly," and I sat for some while hesitating with a great fear very cold at my heart. That door was opening fast. Should I push it open, wide? With one bold thrust of the hand I could do it—if I would. But should I see clearly into the room—so clearly that I could not mistake a single thing I saw. No, I would go on, gently forcing the door back, and all the while accustoming my vision to the gloom.

"Has that shed been used since Cullen Mayle was driven away?"

"No."

"You are certain? Oh, be certain, very certain, before you speak."

Dick looked at me in surprise, as well he might; for I have no doubt my voice betrayed something of the fear and pain I felt.

"I am certain."

"Well, then, have you, has any one heard these dead sailormen making merry—God save the mark —since that shed has been disused?"

Dick thought with considerable effort before he answered. But it did not matter; I was certain what his answer would be.

"I have never heard them," he said.

"Nor have met others who have?"

"No," said he, after a second deliberation, "I don't remember any one who has."

"From the time Cullen Mayle left Tresco to the night when we crossed the Down to Merchant's Rock? There's one thing more. Cullen was in league with the Brittany smugglers. He would be in league, then, with smugglers from Penzance, who would put him over to Tresco secretly, if he needed it?"

THE LOST KEY IS FOUND

"He was very good friends with all smugglers," said Dick.

"Then," said I, rising from the ground, "we will sail back, Dick, to Tresco, and have another look into that shed."

I made him steer the boat eastwards and land behind the point of the old Grimsby Harbour, on which the Block House stands, and out of sight of Merchant's Point. It was not that I did not wish to be seen by any one in that house. But—but— well, I did not wish at that moment to land near it —to land where a voice now grown familiar might call to me.

From the Block House we struck up through Dolphin Town on to the empty hill, and so came to the shed. I pushed open the door and went in. Dick followed me timidly.

The floor was of stone. I had been thinking of that as we sailed across from St. Helen's. I had been thinking, too, that when I was carried into the inner room the door of the partition was jambed against the floor, that Roper had kicked it open, and that, as it yielded, I had heard some iron thing spring from beneath it and jingle across the floor. That iron thing was, undoubtedly, the key which I held in my hand.

I placed it again under the door. There was a fairly strong wind blowing. I told Dick to set the outer door wide open to the wind, which he did. And immediately the inner door began to swing backwards and forwards in the draught. But it dragged the key with it, and it dragged the key over the stone floor. The shed was filled with a harsh, shrill, rasping sound, which set one's fingernails on edge. I set my hand to the door and swung it more quickly backwards and forwards. The harsh sound rose to a hideous inhuman grating screech.

"There are your dead sailormen, Dick," said I. "It was Cullen Mayle who took the key from your door on the night I landed on Tresco—Cullen Mayle, who had my horse to carry him on the road and smuggler friends at Penzance to carry him over the sea. It was Cullen Mayle who was in this shed that night, and used his old trick to scare people from his hiding-place. It was Cullen Mayle who was first in the Abbey burial ground. No doubt Cullen Mayle has that cross. And it was Cullen Mayle whom the woman—— But, there, enough."

The door was wide open now, and this key had opened it. I could see everything clearly. My eyes were, indeed, now accustomed to the gloom—so accustomed that, as I stepped from the shed, all the sunlight seemed struck out of the world.

It was all clear. Helen Mayle had come up to the shed that night. She had told Cullen of the stick in the coffin—yes, she must have done that. She told him of the men who watched. What more had passed between them I could not guess, but she had come back with despair in her heart, and, in the strength of her despair, had walked late at night into his room—with that silk noose in her hand.

That she loved him—that was evident. But why could she not have been frank with me? Cullen had spoken with her, had been warned by her, had left the island since. Why had she kept up this pretence of anxiety on his account, of fear that he was in distress, of dread lest he return unwitting of his peril and fall into Glen's hand? Clutterbuck's word "duplicity" came stinging back to me.

I sent Dick away to sail the boat back to Merchant's Point, and lay for a long while on the open hillside, while the sun sank and evening came. It was only yesterday that she had played in her garden upon the violin. I had felt that I knew her really for the first time as she sat with her pale face gleaming purely through the darkness. Why could she not have been frank to me? The question assailed me; I cried it out. Surely there was some answer, an answer which would preserve my picture of her in her tangled garden, untarnished within my memories. Surely, surely! And how could such deep love mate with duplicity?

I put the scarf into my pocket, and crossed the hill again and came down to Merchant's Point. I could not make up my mind to go in. How could I speak of that night when I slept in Cullen Mayle's bedroom? I lay now upon the gorse watching the bright windows. Now I went down to the sea and its kindly murmurings. And at last, about ten o'clock of the night, a white figure came slowly from the porch and stood beside me.

"You have been here—how long?—I have watched you," she said very gently. "What is it? Why didn't you come in?"

I took both her hands in mine and looked into her eyes.

"Will you be frank with me if I do?"

"Why, yes," she said, and her face was all wonder and all concern. "You hurt me—no, not your hands, but your distrust."

CHAPTER XVI

AN UNSATISFACTORY EXPLANATION

WE went into the house, but no farther than the hall. For the moment we were come there she placed herself in front of me. I remember that the door of the house was never shut, and through the opening I could see a shoulder of the hill and the stars above it, and hear the long roar of the waves upon the beach.

"We are good friends, I hope, you and I," she said. "Plain speech is the privilege of such friendship. Speak, then, as though you were speaking to a man. Wherein have I not been frank with you?"

There must be, I thought, some explanation which would free her from all suspicion of deceit. Else, how could she speak with so earnest a tongue or look with eyes so steady?

"As man to man, then," I answered, "I am grieved I was not told that Cullen Mayle had

UNSATISFACTORY EXPLANATION 239

come secretly to Tresco and had thence escaped."

"Cullen!" she said, in a wondering voice. "He was on Tresco! Where?"

I constrained myself to answer patiently.

"In the Abbey grounds, on St. Helen's Island, and—" I paused, thinking, nay hoping, that even at this eleventh hour she would speak, she would explain. But she kept silence, nor did her eyes ever waver from my face.

—"And," I continued, "on Castle Down."

"There!" she exclaimed, and added, thoughtfully, "Yes, there he would be safe. But when was Cullen upon Tresco? When?"

So the deception was to be kept up.

"On the night," I answered, "when I first came to Merchant's Point."

She looked at me for a little without a word, and I could imagine that it was difficult for her to hit upon an opportune rejoinder. There was one question, however, which might defer her acknowledgments of her concealments, and, to be sure, she asked it:

"How do you know that?" and before I could answer, she added another, which astonished me by its assurance. "When did you find out?"

I told her, I trust with patience, of the key and the various steps by which I had found out. "And as to when," I said, "it was this afternoon."

At that she gave a startled cry, and held out a trembling hand towards me.

"Had you known," she cried, "had you known only yesterday that Cullen had come and had safely got him back, you would have been spared all you went through last night!"

"What I went through last night!" I exclaimed, passionately. "Oh, that is of small account to me, and I beg you not to suffer it to trouble your peace. But—I do not say had I known yesterday, I say had I been *told* yesterday —I should have been spared a very bitter disappointment."

"I do not understand," she said, and again she put out her hand towards me and drew it in and stretched it out again with an appearance of distress to which even at that moment I felt myself softening. However, I took no heed of the hand. "In some way you blame me, but I do not understand."

"You would, perhaps, find it easier to understand if you were at the pains to remember that on the night I landed upon Tresco, I came over

Castle Down and past the shed to Merchant's Point."

"Well?" and she spoke with more coldness, as though her pride made her stubborn in defiance. No doubt she was unaware that I was close to her that night. It remained for me to reveal that, and God knows I did it with no sense of triumph, but only a great sadness.

"As I stood in the darkness a little this side of the shed, a girl hurried down the hill from it. She was dressed in white, so that I could make no mistake. On the other hand, my dark coat very likely made me difficult to see. The girl passed me, and so closely that her frock brushed against my hand. Now, can you name the girl?"

She looked at me with the same stubbornness.

"No," she said, "I cannot."

"On the other hand," said I, "I can. One circumstance enables me to be certain. I slipped on the grass that night, and catching hold of a bush of gorse pricked my hand."

"Yes, I remember that."

"I pricked my hand a minute or two before the girl passed me. As I say, she brushed against my hand, which was bleeding, and the next day

I saw the blood smirched upon a white frock—and who wore it, do you think?"

"I did," she answered.

"Ah! Then you own it. You will own too that I have some cause of discontentment in that you have played with me, whose one thought was to serve you like an honest gentleman."

And at that the stubbornness, the growing resentment at my questions, died clean out of her face.

"You would have!" she cried eagerly. "You would indeed have cause for more than discontent had I played with you. But you do not mean that. You cannot think that I would use any trickeries with you. Oh! take back your words! For indeed they hurt me. You are mistaken here. I wore the frock, but it was not I who was on Castle Down that night. It was not I who brushed past you——"

"And the stain?" I asked.

"How it came there I do not know," she said. "But this I do know,—it was not your hand that marked it. I never knew that Cullen was on Tresco. I never saw him, much less spoke to him. You will believe that? No! Why should I have kept it secret if I had?" and her head drooped as she saw that still I did not believe.

There was silence between us. She stood without changing her attitude, her head bent, her hands nervously clasping and unclasping. The wind came through the open door into the hall. Once in the silence Helen caught her breath; it was as though she checked a sob; and gradually a thought came into my mind which would serve to explain her silence—which would, perhaps, justify it—which, at all events, made of it a mistaken act of kindness. So I spoke with all gentleness—and with a little remorse, too, for the harshness I had shown:

"You said we were good friends, you hoped; and, for my part, I can say that the words were aptly chosen. I am your friend—your good *friend*. You will understand? I want you also to understand that it was not even so much as friendship which brought me down to Tresco. It was Dick's sturdy example, it was my utter weariness, and some spark of shame Dick kindled in me. I was living, though upon my soul *living* is not the word, in one tiresome monotony of disgraceful days. I had made my fortune, and in the making had somehow unlearnt how fitly to enjoy it."

"But this I know," interrupted Helen, now lifting her face to me.

"I never told you."

"But my violin told me. Do you remember? I wanted to know you through and through, to the heart's core. So I took my violin and played to you in the garden. And your face spoke in answer. So I knew you."

It was strange. This confession she made with a blush and a great deal of confusion—a confession of a trick if you will, but a trick to which no one could object, by which anyone might be flattered. But that other more serious duplicity she could deny with an unwavering assurance!

"You know then," I went on. "It makes it easier for me. I want you to understand then that it was to serve myself I came, and I do verily believe that I have served myself better than I have served you. Why, I did not even know what you were like. I did not inquire of Clutterbuck, he drew no picture of you to persuade me to my journey. Thus then there is no reason why you should be silent concerning Cullen out of any consideration for me."

She looked at me in perplexity. My hint had not sufficed. I must make myself more clear.

"I have no doubt," I continued, "that you have seen. No doubt I might have been more circumspect. No doubt I have betrayed myself this last day. But, believe me, you are under no debt to me. If I can bring Cullen Mayle back to you, I will not harbour a thought of jealousy."

Did she understand? I could not be sure. But I saw her whole face brighten and smile—it was as though a glory shone upon it—and her figure straighten with a sort of pride. Did she understand at the last that she need practise no concealments? But she said nothing, she waited for me to say what more I had to say. Well, I could make the matter yet more plain.

"Besides," I said, "I knew—I knew very well before I set out from London, Clutterbuck told me. So that it is my own fault, you see, if when I came here I took no account of what he told me. And even so, believe me, I do not regret the fault."

"Lieutenant Clutterbuck!" she exclaimed, with something almost of alarm. "He told you what?"

"He told me of a night very like this. You were standing in this hall, very likely as you stand now, and the door was open and the breeze and the sound of the sea came through the open door as it does now. Only where I stand Cullen Mayle stood, asking you to follow him out through the world. And you would have followed, you did indeed begin to follow——"

So far I had got when she broke in passionately, with her eyes afire!

"It is not true! How can men speak such lies? Lieutenant Clutterbuck! I know—he told me the same story. It would have been much easier, so much franker, had he said outright he was tired of his—friendship for me and wished an end to it. I should have liked him the better had he been so frank. But that he should tell you the same story Oh! it is despicable—and you believe it?" she challenged me. "You believe that story. You believe, too, I went to a trysting with Cullen on Castle Down, the night you came, and kept it secret from you and let you run the peril of your life. You will have it, in a word, whatever I may say or do," and she wrung her hands with a queer helplessness. "You will have it that I love him. Pity, a sense of injustice, a feeling that I wrongly possess what is rightly his—these things you will not allow can move me. No, I must love him."

UNSATISFACTORY EXPLANATION 247

"Have I not proof you do?" I answered. "Not from Clutterbuck, but from yourself. Have I not proof into what despair your love could throw you?" And I took from my pocket the silk scarf. "Where did I get this?"

She took it from my hands, while her face softened. She drew it through her fingers, and a smile parted her lips. She raised her eyes to me with a certain shyness, and she answered shyly:

"Yet you say you were not curious to know anything of me in London before you started to the West."

The answer was no answer at all. I repeated my question:

"How do I come to have that scarf?"

"I can but guess," she said; "I did not know that Lieutenant Clutterbuck possessed it. But it could be no one else. You asked it of Lieutenant Clutterbuck in London."

For a moment I could not believe that I had heard a right. I stared at her. It was impossible that any woman could carry effrontery to so high a pitch. But she repeated her words.

"Lieutenant Clutterbuck gave it to you no

doubt in London, and—will you tell me?—I should like to know. Did you ask him for it?"

Should I strip away this pretence? Should I compel her to own where I found it and how I came by it? But it seemed not worth while. I turned on my heel without a word, and went straight out through the open door and on to the hillside.

And so this was the second night which I spent in the gorse of Castle Down. One moment I was hot to go back to London and speak to no woman for the rest of my days. The next I was all for finding Cullen Mayle and heaping coals of fire upon Helen's head. The coals of fire carried the day in the end.

As morning broke I walked down to the Palace Inn fully resolved. I would search for Cullen Mayle until I found him. I would bring him back. I would see him married to Helen from a dark corner in St. Mary's Church, and when the pair were properly unhappy and miserable, as they would undoubtedly become—I was very sorry, but miserable they would be—why then I would send her a letter. The writing in the letter should be "Ha! ha!"—not a word more, not even a signature, but just " Ha! ha!" on a blank sheet of paper.

But, as I have said, I had grown very young these last few days.

CHAPTER XVII

CULLEN MAYLE COMES HOME

THE search was entirely unsuccessful. Through the months of November and December I travelled hither and thither, but I had no hint as to Cullen Mayle's whereabouts; and towards the end of the year I took passage in a barque bound for St. Mary's, where I landed the day before Christmas and about the fall of the dusk. It was my intention to cross over that night to Tresco and report my ill-success, which I was resolved to do with a deal of stateliness. I was also curious to know whether Peter Tortue was still upon the island.

But as I walked along the street of Hugh Town to the "Dolphin" Inn, by the Customs House, a band of women dancing and shouting, with voices extraordinarily hoarse, swept round the corner. I fell plump amongst them, and discovered they were men masquerading as women. Moreover, they stopped me, and were for believing that I was a woman masquerading as a man; and, indeed, when they had let me go I did come upon a party of girls dressed up for sea captains and the like, who swaggered, counterfeiting a manly walk, and drawing their hangers upon one another with a great show of spirit.

The reason of these transformations was explained to me at the "Dolphin." It seems that they call this sort of amusement "a goose-dancing," and the young people exercise it in these islands at Christmas time. I was told that it would be impossible for me to hire a boatman to put me over to Tresco that night; so I made the best of the matter, and to pass the time stepped out again into the street, which was now lighted up with many torches and crowded with masqueraders. They went dancing and singing from house to house; the women paid their addresses with an exaggeration of courtly manners to the men, who, dressed in the most uncouth garments that could be devised, received them with a droll shyness and modesty, and altogether, what with liquor and music, the festival went with a deal of noise and spirit. But in the midst of it one of these false women, with a great bonnet pulled forward over her face, clapped a hand upon my shoulder and said in my ear:

"Mr. Berkeley, I hope you have been holding better putt cards of late;" and would have run on, but I caught him by the arm.

"Mr. Featherstone," said I, "you stole my horse; I have a word to say to you."

"I have not the time to listen," said he, wrenching his arm free as he flung himself into the thick of the crowd. I kept close upon his heels, however, which he perceived, and drawing into a corner he suddenly turned round upon me.

"Your horse is dead," said he. "I very much regret it; but I will pay you, for I have but now come into an inheritance. I will pay you for it to-morrow."

"I did not follow you to speak of the horse, or to Mr. Featherstone at all, but to Mr. Cullen Mayle."

"You know me?" he exclaimed, looking about him lest the name should have been overheard.

"And have news for you," I added. "Will you follow me to the 'Dolphin?'"

I went back to the inn, secured from my host a room where we could be private, and went out to the door. Cullen Mayle was waiting; he followed me quickly in, hiding his face so that no one could recognise him, and when the door was shut—

"How in the world did you come to know of my name?" said he. "I cannot think, but I shall be obliged if you will keep it secret for a day or so, for I am not sure but what I may have some inconvenient friends among these islands."

"Those inconvenient friends are all gone but one," said I.

"You know that too," he exclaimed. "Indeed, Mr. Berkeley, you seem to be very well acquainted with my affairs; but I cannot regret it, since you give me such comforting news. Only one of my inconvenient friends left! Why, I am a match for one—I think I may say so without vaunting—so it seems I can come to Tresco and take up my inheritance."

With that he began briskly to unhook the cotton dress which he had put on over his ordinary clothes.

"Inheritance!" said I. "You mentioned the word before. I do not understand."

"Oh," said he, "it is a long story and a melancholy. My father drove me from the house, and bequeathed his fortune to an adopted daughter."

"Yes," said I quickly, "I know that too."

"Indeed!" and he stopped his toilette to stare at me. "Perhaps you are aware then that Helen Mayle, conscious of my father's injustice, bequeathed it again to me."

"Yes, but—but—you spoke of an immediate inheritance."

"Ah," said he, coolly, "there is something, then, I can inform you of. Helen Mayle is dead."

"What's that?" I cried, and started to my feet. I did not understand. I was like a man struck by a bullet, aware dimly that some hurt has come to him, but not yet conscious of the pain, not yet sensible of the wound.

"Hush!" said Cullen Mayle, and untying a string at his waist he let his dress fall about his feet. "It is most sad. Not for the world would I have come into this inheritance at such a cost. You knew Helen Mayle, perhaps?" he asked, with a shrewd glance at me. "A girl very staunch, very true, who would never forget a *friend.*" He emphasised that word "friend" and made it of a greater significance. "Indeed, I am not sure, but I must think it was because she could not forget a—friend that, alas! she died."

I was standing stupefied. I heard the words he

spoke, but gave them at this moment no meaning. I was trying to understand the one all-important fact.

"Dead!" I babbled. "Helen Mayle—dead!"

"Yes, and in the strangest, pitiful way. I cannot think of it, without the tears come into my eyes. The news came to me but lately, and you will perhaps excuse me on that account." His voice broke as he spoke; there were tears, too, in his eyes. I wondered, in a dull way, whether after all he had really cared for her. "But how comes it that you knew her?" he asked.

I sat down upon a chair and told him—of Dick Parmiter's coming to London, of my journey into the West. I told him how I had come to recognise him at the inn; and as I spoke the comprehension of Helen's death crept slowly into my mind, so that I came to a stop and could speak no more.

"You were on your way to Tresco," said he, "when we first met. Then you know that she is dead?"

"No," I answered. "When did she die?"

"On the sixth of October," said he.

I do not think that I should have paid great heed to his words, but something in his voice—

an accent of alarm—roused me. I lifted my eyes and saw that he was watching me with a singular intentness.

"The sixth of October," I repeated vaguely, and then I broke into a laugh, so harsh and hysterical that it seemed quite another voice than mine. "Your news is false," I cried; "she is not dead! Why, I did not leave Tresco till the end of October, and she was alive then and no sign of any malady. The sixth of October! No, indeed, she did not die upon that day."

"Are you sure?" he exclaimed.

"Sure?" said I. "I have the best of reasons to be sure; for it was on the sixth of October that I first set foot in Tresco," and at once Cullen Mayle sprang up and shook me by the hand.

"Here is the bravest news," he said. His whole face was alight; he could not leave hold of my hand. "Mr. Berkeley, I may thank God that I spoke to you to-night. 'Helen!'"—and he lingered upon the name. "Upon my word, it would take little more to unman me. So you landed on the sixth of October. But are you sure of the date?" he asked with earnestness. "I borrowed your horse but a few days before. You would hardly have travelled so quickly."

"I travelled by sea with a fair wind," said I. "It was the sixth of October. Could I forget it? Why, that very night I crossed Castle Down to Merchant's Point; that very night I entered the house. Dick Parmiter showed me a way. I crept into the house, and slept in your bedroom——"

I had spoken so far without a notion of the disclosure to which my words were leading me. I was not looking at Cullen Mayle, but on to the ground, else very likely I might have read it upon his face. But now in an instant the truth of the matter was clear to me. For as I said, "I slept in your bedroom," he uttered one loud cry, leapt to his feet, and stood over against me, very still and quiet. I had sufficient wit not to raise my head and betray this new piece of knowledge. That sad and pitiful death on the sixth of October, of which he had heard with so deep a pain—he had never heard it, he had *planned* it, and the plan miscarried. He knew why, now, and so was standing in front of me very still and quiet. He had seen Helen that night on Castle Down; there, no doubt, she had told him how in her will she had disposed of her inheritance; and he had persuaded her, working on her generosity—with what prepared speeches of despair!—to that strange, dark act which it had been my good fortune to interrupt. It was clear to me. The very choice of that room, wherein alone secrecy was possible, made it clear. He had suggested to her the whole cunning plan; and a moment ago I had almost been deceived to believe his expressions of distress sincere!

"I told you I was nearly unmanned," I heard him say; "and you see even so I underrated the strength of my relief, so that the mere surprise of your ingenious shift to get a lodging took my breath away."

He resumed his seat, and I, having now composed my face, raised it full to him. I have often wondered since whether, as he stood above me, motionless and silent during those few moments, I was in any danger.

"Yes," said I, "it was no doubt surprising."

This, however, was not the only surprise I was to cause Cullen Mayle that night.

He proposed immediately that we should cross to Tresco together, and on my objecting that we should get no one to carry us over—

"Oh," said he, "I have convenient friends in Scilly as well as inconvenient." He looked out of the window. "The tide is high, and washes the steps at the back of the inn. Do you wait here upon the steps. I will have a boat there in less than half an hour;" and on the word he hooked up his dress again and got him out of the inn.

I waited upon the steps as he bade me. Behind me were the lights and the uproar of the street; in front, the black water and the cool night; and still further, out of sight, the island of Tresco, the purple island of bracken and gorse, resonant with the sea.

In a little I heard a ripple of water, and the boat swam to the steps. I was careful as we sailed across the road to say nothing to Cullen Mayle which would provoke his suspicion. I did not even allow him to see I was aware that he himself had been upon Tresco on the sixth of October. It was not difficult for me to keep silence. For as the water splashed and seethed under the lee of the boat, and Tresco drew nearer, I had to consider what I should do in the light of my new knowledge. It would have been so much easier had only Helen been frank with me.

Tresco dimly loomed up out of the darkness.

"By the way," said Cullen Mayle, who had

been silent too, "you said that one of the watchers had remained. It will be George Glen, I suppose."

"No," I answered. "It is a Frenchman, Peter Tortue," and by the mere mention of the name I surprised Cullen Mayle again that evening. It is true that this time he uttered no exclamation, and did not start from his seat. But the boat shot up into the wind and got into irons, as the saying is, so that I knew his hand had left the tiller. But he said nothing until we were opposite to the Blockhouse, and then he asked in a low trembling voice :

" Did you say Peter Tortue?"

"Yes."

There was another interval of silence. Then he put another question and in the same tone of awe :

"A young fellow, less than my years——"

"No. The young fellow's father," said I. "A man of sixty years. I think I should be wary of him."

"Why?"

"He said, 'I am looking, not for the cross, but for a man to nail upon the cross,' and he meant his words, every syllable."

Again we fell to silence, and so crossed the Old Grimsby Harbour and rounded its northern point. The lights of the house were in view at last. They shot out across the darkness in thin lines of light and wavered upon the black water lengthening and shortening with the slight heave of the waves. When they shortened, I wondered whether they beckoned me to the house; when they lengthened out, were they fingers which pointed to us to be gone?

"Since you know so much, Mr. Berkeley," whispered Cullen Mayle, "perhaps you can tell me whether Glen secured the cross."

"No, he failed in that."

"I felt sure he would," said Cullen with a chuckle, and he ran the boat aground, not on the sand before the house but on the bank beneath the garden hedge. We climbed through the hedge; two windows blazed upon the night, and in the room sat Helen Mayle close by the fire, her violin on a table at her side and the bow swinging in her hand. I stepped forward and rapped at the window. She walked across the room and set her face to the pane, shutting out the light from her eyes with her hands. She saw us standing side by side. Instantly she drew down the blinds and came to the door, and over the grass towards us. She came first to me with her hand outstretched.

"It is you," she said gently, and the sound of her voice was wonderful in my ears. I had taken her hand before I was well aware what I did.

"Yes," said I.

"You have come back. I never thought you would. But you have come."

"I have brought back Cullen Mayle," said I, as indifferently as I could, and so dropped her hand. She turned to Cullen then.

"Quick," she said. "You must come in."

We went inside the door.

"It is some years since I trod these flags," said Cullen. "Well, I am glad to come home, though it is only as an outcast; and indeed, Helen, I have not the right even to call it home."

It was as cruel a remark as he could well have made, seeing at what pains the girl had been, and still was, to restore that home to him. That it hurt her I knew very well, for I heard her, in the darkness of the passage, draw in her breath through her clenched teeth. Cullen walked along the passage and through the hall.

"Lock the door," Helen said to me, and I did lock it. "Now drop the bar."

When that was done we walked together into the hall, where she stopped.

"Look at me," she said, "please!" and I obeyed her.

"You have come back," she repeated. "You do not, then, any longer believe that I deceived you?"

"There is a reason why I have come back," I answered. It was a reason which I could not give to her. I was resolved not to suffer her to lie at the mercy of Cullen Mayle. Fortunately, she did not think to ask me to be particular about the reason. But she beat her hands once or twice together, and—

"You still believe it, then!" she cried. "With these two months to search and catch and hold the truth, you still hold me in the same contempt as when you turned your back on me and walked out through that door?"

"No, no!" I exclaimed. "Contempt! That never entered into any thought I ever had of you. Make sure of that!"

"Yet you believe I tricked you. How can you believe that, and yet spare me your contempt!"

"I am no philosopher. It is the truth I tell you," I answered, simply; and the face of Cullen Mayle appeared at the doorway of the parlour, so that no more was said.

CHAPTER XVIII

MY PERPLEXITIES ARE EXPLAINED

THERE is no need for me to tell at any length the conversation that passed between the three of us that night. Cullen Mayle spoke frankly of his journey to the Sierra Leone River.

"Mr. Berkeley," he said, "already knows so much, that I doubt it would not be of any avail to practise mysteries with him. And besides there is no need, for, if I mistake not, Mr. Berkeley can keep a secret as well as any man."

He spoke very politely, but with a keen eye on me to notice whether I should show any confusion or change colour. But I made as though I attached no significance to his words beyond mere urbanity. He told us how he made his passage to the Guinea Coast as a sailor before the mast, and then fell in with George Glen. It seemed prudent to counterfeit a friendly opinion that the cross would be enough for all. But when they discovered the cross was gone from its hiding place, he took the first occasion to give them the slip.

"For I had no doubt that my father had been beforehand," said he. "Had I possessed more wisdom, I might have known as much when I heard him from my bed refuse his assistance to George Glen, and so saved myself an arduous and a perilous adventure. For my father, was he never so rich, was not the man to turn his back on the King of Portugal's cross."

Of his father, Cullen spoke with good nature and a certain hint of contempt; and he told us much which he had learned from George Glen. "He went by the name of Kennedy," said Cullen, "but they called him 'Crackers' for the most part. He was not on the *Royal Fortune* at the time when Roberts was killed, so that he was never taken prisoner with the rest, nor did he creep out of Cape Corse Castle like George Glen."

"Then he was never tried or condemned," said Helen, who plainly found some relief in that thought.

"No!" answered Cullen, with a chuckle. "But why? He played rob-thief—a good game, but it requires a skilled player. I would never have believed Adam had the skill. Roberts put him in command of a sloop called the *Ranger*, which he had taken in the harbour of Bahia, and when he put out to sea on that course which brought him into conjunction with the *Swallow*, he left the *Ranger* behind in Whydah Bay. And what does Adam do but haul up his anchor as soon as Roberts was out of sight, and, being well content with his earnings, make sail for Maryland, where the company was disbanded. I would I had known that on the day we quarrelled. Body o' me, but I would have made the old man quiver. Well, Adam came home to England, settled at Bristol, where he married, and would no doubt have remained there till his death, had he not fallen in with one of his old comrades on the quay. That frightened him, so he come across to Tresco, thinking to be safe. And safe he was for twenty years, until George Glen nosed him out."

Thereupon, Cullen, from relating his adventures, turned to questions asking for word of this man and that whom he had known before he went away. These questions of course he put to Helen, and not once did he let slip a single allusion to the meeting he had had with her in the shed on Castle Down. For that silence on his part I was well prepared; the man was versed in secrecy. But Helen showed a readiness no whit inferior; she never hesitated, never caught a word back. They spoke together as though the last occasion when they had met was the night, now four years and a half ago, when Adam Mayle stood at the head of the stairs and drove his son from the house. One thing in particular I learned from her, the negro had died a month ago.

It was my turn when the gossip of the islands had been exhausted, and I had to tell over again of my capture by Glen and the manner of my escape. I omitted, however, all mention of an earlier visitant to the Abbey burial grounds, and it was to this omission that I owed a confirmation of my conviction that Cullen Mayle was the visitant. For when I came to relate how George Glen and his band sailed away towards France without the cross, he said:

"If I could find that cross, I might perhaps think I had some right to it. It is yours, Helen, to be sure, by law, and——"

She interrupted him, as she was sure to do, with a statement that the cross and everything else was for him to dispose of as he thought fit. But he was magnanimous to a degree.

"The cross, Helen, nothing but the cross, if I can find it. I have a thought which may help me to it. 'Three chains east of the east window in south aisle of St. Helen's Church.' Those were the words, I think."

"Yes," said I.

"And Glen measured the distance correctly?"

"To an inch."

"Well, what if—it is a mere guess, but a likely one, I presume to think,—what if the chains were Cornish chains? There would be a difference of a good many feet, a difference of which George Glen would be unaware. You see I trust you, Mr. Berkeley. I fancy that I can find that cross upon St. Helen's Island."

"I have no doubt you will," said I.

Cullen rose from his chair.

"It grows late, Helen," said he, "and I have kept you from your sleep with my gossiping." He turned to me. "But, Mr. Berkeley, you perhaps will join me in a pipe and a glass of rum? My father had a good store of rum, which in those days I despised, but I have learnt the taste for it."

His proposal suited very well with my determination to keep a watch that night over Helen's safety, and I readily agreed.

"You will sleep in your old room, Cullen," she said, " and you, Mr. Berkeley, in the room next to it;" and that arrangement suited me very well. Helen wished us both good-night, and left us together.

We went up into Mayle's cabin and Cullen mixed the rum, which I only sipped. So it was not the rum. I cannot, in fact, remember at all feeling any drowsiness or desire to sleep. I think if I had felt that desire coming over me I should have shaken it off; it would have warned me to keep wide awake. But I was not sensible of it at all; and I remember very vividly the last thing of which I was conscious. That was Cullen Mayle's great silver watch which he held by a ribbon and twirled this way and that as he chatted to me. He spun it with great quickness, so that it flashed in the light of the candle like a mirror, and at once held and tired the eyes. I was conscious of this, I say, and of nothing more until gradually I understood that some one was shaking me by the shoulders and rousing me from sleep. I opened my eyes and saw that it was Helen Mayle who had disturbed me.

PERPLEXITIES EXPLAINED

It took me a little time to collect my wits. I should have fallen asleep again had she not hindered me; but at last I was sufficiently roused to realise that I was still in the cabin, but that Cullen Mayle had gone. A throb of anger at my weakness in so letting him steal a march quickened me and left me wide awake. Helen Mayle was however in the room, plainly then she had suffered no harm by my negligence. She was at this moment listening with her ear close to the door, so that I could not see her face.

"What has happened?" I asked, and she flung up her hand with an imperative gesture to be silent.

After listening for a minute or so longer she turned towards me, and the aspect of her face filled me with terror.

"In God's name what has happened, Helen?" I whispered. For never have I seen such a face, so horror-stricken—no, and I pray that I never may again, though the face be a stranger's and not one of which I carried an impression in my heart.

Yet she spoke with a natural voice.

"You took so long to wake!" said she.

"What o'clock is it?" I asked.

"Three. Three of the morning; but speak

low, or rather listen! Listen, and while you listen look at me, so that I may know." She seated herself on a chair close to mine, and leant forward, speaking in a whisper. "On the night of the sixth of October I went to the shed on Castle Down and had word with Cullen Mayle. Returning I passed you, brushed against you. So much you have maintained before. But listen, listen! That night you climbed into Cullen's bedroom and fell asleep, and you woke up in the dark middle of the night."

"Stop! stop!" I whispered, and seized her hands in mine. Horror was upon me now, and a hand of ice crushing down my heart. I did not reason or argue at that moment. I knew—her face told me—she had been after all ignorant of what she had done that night. "Stop; not a word more—there is no truth in it."

"Then there is truth in it," she answered, "for you know what I have not yet told you. It is true, then—your waking up—the silk noose! My God! my God!" and all the while she spoke in a hushed whisper, which made her words ten times more horrible, and sat motionless as stone. There was not even a tremor in the hands I held; they lay like ice in mine.

"How do you know?" I said. "But I would have spared you this! You did not know, and I doubted you. Of course—of course you did not know. Good God! Why could not this secret have lain hid in me? I would have spared you the knowledge of it. I would have carried it down safe with me into my grave."

Her face hardened as I spoke. She looked down and saw that I held her hands; she plucked them free.

"You would have kept the secret safe," she said, steadily. "You liar! You told it this night to Cullen Mayle."

Her words struck me like a blow in the face. I leaned back in my chair. She kept her eyes upon my face.

"I—told it—to Cullen Mayle?" I repeated.

She nodded her head.

"To-night?"

"Here in this room. My door was open. I overheard."

"I did not know I told him," I exclaimed; and she laughed horribly and leaned back in the chair.

All at once I understood, and the comprehension wrapped me in horror. The horror passed from me to her, though as yet she did not understand. She looked as though the world yawned wide beneath her feet. "Oh!" she moaned, and, "Hush!" said I, and I leaned forward towards her. "I did not know, just as you did not know that you went to the shed on Castle Down, that you brushed against me as you returned,—just as you did not know of what happened thereafter."

She put her hands to her head and shivered.

"Just as you did not know that four years ago when Cullen Mayle was turned from the door, he bade you follow him, and you obeyed," I continued. "This is Cullen Mayle's work—devil's work. He spun his watch to dazzle you four years ago; he did the same to-night, and made me tell him why his plan miscarried. Plan!" and at last I understood. I rose to my feet; she did the same. "Yes, plan! You told him you had bequeathed everything to him. He knew that to-night when I met him at St. Mary's. How did he know it unless you told him on Castle Down? He bade you go home, enter his room, where no one would hear you, and—don't you see? Helen! Helen!"

I took her in my arms, and she put her hands upon my shoulders and clung to them.

"I have heard of such things in London," said I. "Some men have this power to send you to sleep and make you speak or forget at their pleasure; and some have more power than this, for they can make you do when you have waked up what they have bidden you to do while you slept, and afterwards forget the act;" and suddenly Helen started away from me, and raised her finger.

We both stood and listened.

"I can hear nothing," I whispered.

She looked over her shoulder to the door. I motioned her not to move. I walked noiselessly to the door, and noiselessly turned the handle. I opened the door for the space of an inch; all was quiet in the house.

"Yet I heard a voice," she said, and the next moment I heard it too.

The candles were alight. I crossed the room and squashed them with the palm of my hand. I was not a moment too soon, for even as I did so I heard the click of a door handle, and then a creak of the hinges, and a little afterwards—footsteps.

A hand crept into mine; we waited in the darkness, holding our breath. The footsteps came down the passage to the door behind which we stood and passed on. I expected that they would be going towards the room in which Helen slept. I waited for them to cease that I might follow and catch Cullen Mayle, damned by some bright proof in his hand of a murderous intention. But they did not cease; they kept on and on. Surely he must have reached the room. At last the footsteps ceased. I opened the door cautiously and heard beneath me in the hall a key turn in a lock.

A great hope sprang up in me. Suppose that since his plan had failed, and since Tortue waited for him on Tresco, he had given up! Suppose that he was leaving secretly, and for good and all! If that supposition could be true! I prayed that it might be true, and as if in answer to my prayer I saw below me where the hall door should be a thin slip of twilight. This slip broadened and broadened. The murmur of the waves became a roar. The door was opening—no, now it was shutting again; the twilight narrowed to a slip and disappeared altogether.

"Listen," said I, and we heard footsteps on the stone tiles of the porch.

"Oh, he is gone!" said Helen, in an indescribable accent of relief.

"Yes, gone," said I. "See, the door of his room is open."

I ran down the passage and entered the room. Helen followed close behind me.

"He is gone," I repeated. The words sounded too pleasant to be true. I approached the bed and flung aside the curtains. I stooped forward over the bed.

"Helen," I cried, and aloud, "out of the room! Quick! Quick!"

For the words *were* too pleasant to be true. I flung up my arm to keep her back. But I was too late. She had already seen. She had approached the bed, and in the dim twilight she had seen. She uttered a piercing scream, and fell against me in a dead swoon.

For the man who had descended the stairs and unlocked the door was not Cullen Mayle.

CHAPTER XIX

THE LAST

MESMER at this date was a youth of twenty-four, but the writings of Van Helmont and Wirdig and G. Maxwell had already thrown more than a glimmering of light upon the reciprocal action of bodies upon each other, and had already demonstrated the existence of a universal magnetic force by which the human will was rendered capable of influencing the minds of others. It was not, however, till seventeen years later—in the year 1775, to be precise—that Mesmer published his famous letter to the Academies of Europe. And by a strange chance it was in the same year that I secured a further confirmation of his doctrines and at the same time an explanation of the one matter concerned with this history of which I was still in ignorance. In a word, I learned at last how young Peter Tortue came by his death.

I did not learn it from his father. That implacable man I never saw after the night when we listened to his footsteps descending the stairs in the darkness. He was gone the next morning from the islands, nor was any trace of him, for all the hue and cry, discovered for a long while—not, indeed, for ten years, when my son, who was then a lad of eight, while playing one day among the rocks of Peninnis Head on St. Mary's, dropped clean out of my sight, or rather out of Helen's sight, for I was deep in a book, and did not raise my head until a cry from my wife startled me.

We ran to the loose pile of boulders where the boy had vanished, and searched and called for a few minutes without any answer. But in the end a voice answered us, and from beneath our feet. It was the boy's voice sure enough, but it sounded hollow, as though it came from the bowels of the earth. By following the sound we discovered at last between the great boulders an interstice, which would just allow a man to slip below ground. This slit went down perpendicularly for perhaps fifteen or twenty feet, but there were sure footholds and one could disappear in a second. At the bottom of this hole was a little cave, very close and dark, in which one could sit or crouch.

On the floor of this cave I picked up a knife, and, bringing it to the light, I recognised the carved blade, which I had seen Tortue once polish upon his thigh in the red light of a candle. The cave, upon inquiry, was discovered to be well known amongst the smugglers, though it was kept a secret by them, and they called it by the curious name of Issachum-Pucchar.

This discovery was made in the year of 1768, and seven years later I chanced to be standing upon the quay at Leghorn when a vessel from Oporto, laden with wine and oil, dropped anchor in the harbour, and her master came ashore. I recognised him at once, although the years had changed him. It was Nathaniel Roper. I followed him up into the town, where he did his business with the shipping agent and thence repaired to a tavern. I entered the tavern, and sitting down over against him at the same table, begged him to oblige me by drinking a glass at my expense, which he declared himself ready to do. "But I cannot tell why you should want to drink with me rather than another," said he.

"Oh! as to that," said I, "we are old acquaintances."

He answered, with an oath or two, that he

could not lay his tongue to the occasion of our meeting.

"You swear very fluently and well," said I. "But you swore yet more fluently, I have no doubt, that morning you sailed away from St. Helen's Island without the Portuguese King's cross."

His face turned the colour of paper, he half rose from his chair and sat down again.

"I was never on Tresco," he stammered.

"Who spoke of Tresco, my friend?" said I, with a laugh. "I made mention of St. Helen's. Yet you were upon Tresco. Have you forgotten? The shed on Castle Down? The Abbey burial ground?" and then he knew me, though for awhile he protested that he did not.

But I persuaded him in the end that I meant no harm to him.

"You were at Sierra Leone with Cullen, maybe," said I. "Tell me how young Peter Tortue came by his death?" and he told me the story which he had before told to old Peter in an alehouse at Wapping.

Peter, it appeared, had not been able to hold his tongue at Sierra Leone. It became known through his chattering that Glen's company and

Cullen Mayle were going up the river in search of treasure, and it was decided for the common good to silence him lest he should grow more particular, and relate what the treasure was and how it came to be buried on the bank of that river. George Glen was for settling the matter with the stab of a knife, but Cullen Mayle would have none of such rough measures.

"I know a better and more delicate way," said he, "a way very amusing too. You shall all laugh to-morrow;" and calling Peter Tortue to him, he betook himself with the whole party to the house of an old buccaneering fellow, John Leadstone, who kept the best house in the settlement, and lived a jovial life in safety, being on very good terms with any pirate who put in. He had, indeed, two or three brass guns before his door, which he was wont to salute the appearance of a black flag with. To his house then the whole gang repaired, and while they were making merry, Cullen Mayle addressed himself with an arduous friendliness to Peter Tortue, taking his watch from his fob and bidding the Frenchman admire it. For a quarter of an hour he busied himself in this way, and then of a sudden in a stern commanding voice he said:

"Stand up in the centre of the room," which Peter Tortue obediently did.

"Now," continued Cullen, with a chuckle to his companions, "I'll show you a trick that will tickle you. Peter," and he turned toward him. "Peter," and he spoke in the softest, friendliest voice, "you talk too much. I'll clap a gag on your mouth, you stinking offal! To-morrow night, my friend, at ten o'clock by my watch, when we are lying in our boat upon the river, you will fall asleep. Do you hear that?"

"Yes," said Peter Tortue, gazing at Mayle.

"At half-past ten, as you sleep, you will feel cramped for room, and you will dangle a leg over the side of the boat in the river. Do you hear that?"

"Yes!"

"Very well," said Cullen. "That will learn you to hold your tongue. Now come back to your chair."

Peter obeyed him again.

"When you wake up," added Cullen, "you will continue to talk of my watch which you so much admire. You will not be aware that any time has passed since you spoke of it before. You can wake up now."

He made some sort of motion with his hands and Peter, whose eyes had all this time been open, said:

"I'll buy a watch as like that as a pea to a pea. First thing I will, as soon as I handle my share."

Cullen Mayle laughed, but he was the only one of that company that did. The rest rather shrank from him as from something devilish, at which, however, he only laughed the louder, being as it seemed flattered by their fear.

The next day the six men started up the river in a long-boat which they borrowed of Leadstone, and sailed all that day until evening when the tide began to fall.

Thereupon Cullen, who held the tiller, steered the boat out of the channel of the river and over the mudbanks, which at high tide were covered to the depth of some feet.

Here all was forest: the great tree-trunks, entwined with all manner of creeping plants, stood up from the smooth oily water, and the roof of branches over head made it already night.

"I have lost my way," said Cullen. "It will not be safe to try to regain the channel until the tide rises. It falls very quickly here, Leadstone tells me, and we should get stuck upon some mudbank. Let us look for a pool where we may lie until the tide rises in the morning."

Accordingly they took their oars and pulled in and out amongst the trees, while Cullen Mayle sounded with the boat-hook for a greater depth of water. The tide fell rapidly; bushes of undergrowth scraped the boat's side, and then Mayle's boathook went down and touched no bottom.

"This will do," said he.

It was nine o'clock by his watch at this time, and the crew without any fire or light made their supper in the boat as best they could. Meanwhile the tide still sank; banks of mud rose out of the black water; the forest stirred, and was filled with a horrible rustling sound, of fish flapping and crabs crawling and scuttering in the slime; and on the pool on which the boat lay every now and then a ripple would cross the water as though a faint wind blew, and a broad black snout would show, and a queer lugubrious cough echo out amongst the tree-trunks.

"Crocodiles, Peter," said Cullen gaily, and he clapped Tortue on the shoulder. "It would not be prudent to take a bath in the pool. Hand the lantern over, Glen!" and when he had the lantern in his hand he looked at his watch.

"Five minutes to ten," said he. "Well, it is not so long to wait."

"Four hours," grumbled Tortue, who was thinking of the tide.

"No, only five minutes, my friend," Cullen corrected him, softly; and sure enough in five minutes Peter stretched himself and complained that he was sleepy.

Cullen laughed with a gentle enjoyment and whistled a tune between his teeth. But the others waited in a sort of paralysis of horror and amazement. Even these hardened men were struck with a cold fear. The suggestions of the place, too, had their effect. Above them was a black roof of leaves, the close air was foul with the odour of things decaying and things decayed, and everywhere about them was perpetually heard the crawling and pattering of the obscene things which lived in the mud.

Peter Tortue stirred in his sleep, and Cullen held up the face of his watch in the light of the lantern so that all in the boat might see. It was half-past ten. Peter lifted his leg over the side and let it fall with a splash in the water. It dangled there for about five minutes, and then the man uttered a loud scream and clutched at the thwart, but the next instant he was dragged over the boat's side.

Roper told me this story, and the horror of it lived again upon his face as he spoke.

"Well," said I, "the father took his revenge. He stabbed Cullen Mayle to the heart as he lay in bed. There is one thing more I would like to know. Can you remember the paper with the directions of the spot where the cross was buried?"

"Yes," said he; "am I likely to forget it?"

"Could you write them out again, word for word and line for line, as they were written?"

"Yes," said he.

I called for a sheet of paper and a pen and ink, and set them before Roper, and he wrote the directions laboriously, and handed the paper back to me. There were only two lines with which I was concerned, and they ran in this order:

"The S aisle of St. Helen's Church. Three chains east by the compass of the east window."

"Are you sure you have made no mistake?" I asked. "This is a facsimile of the paper which you took from the hollow of the stick. Look again!"

I gave it back to him and he scratched his head over it for a little. Then he wrote the directions again upon a second sheet of paper, and when he had written, tore off a corner of the paper.

"Ah!" said I, "that is what I thought." He handed it to me again, and it ran now :—

"The S aisle of S. Helen's Church. Three chains east by the compass of the east window."

On that corner which had been torn a word had been written. I knew the word. It would be "Cornish." I knew, too, who had torn off the corner.

The cross still lies then three Cornish chains east of that window, or should do so. We at all events have not disturbed it, for we do not wish to have continually before our eyes a reminder of those days when the sailors watched the house at Merchant's Point. Even as it is, I start up too often from my sleep in the dark night and peer forward almost dreading again to see the flutter of white at the foot of the bed, and to hear again the sound of some one choking.

THE END.

www.ingramcontent.com/pod-product-compliance
Lightning Source LLC
Chambersburg PA
CBHW032056220426
43664CB00008B/1028